Lucy Kerbel

Lucy Kerbel is the Director of Tonic Theatre. Prior to founding Tonic in 2011, Lucy worked as a theatre director. It was while directing around the UK that she became interested in the question of gender equality in theatre. Recognising the industry would need better support if it were to achieve greater gender balance in its workforces and repertoires, she founded Tonic to go some way towards achieving this. She now heads Tonic's work across theatre, the performing arts and wider creative industries.

Lucy's first book *100 Great Plays for Women* is also published by Nick Hern Books. She is a regular speaker on women in the arts, and is on the board of the Susan Smith Blackburn Prize for women playwrights.

All Change Please

A Practical Guide for Achieving Gender Equality in Theatre

Lucy Kerbel

NICK HERN BOOKS
www.nickhernbooks.co.uk

TONIC THEATRE
www.tonictheatre.co.uk

All Change Please
first published in Great Britain in 2017
by Nick Hern Books Limited,
The Glasshouse, 49a Goldhawk Road, London W12 8QP
in association with Tonic Theatre

Designed and typeset by Nick Hern Books, London
Printed and bound in Great Britain by
CPI Group (UK) Ltd

A CIP catalogue record for this book
is available from the British Library

ISBN 978 1 84842 658 0

MIX
Paper from
responsible sources
FSC® C020471
FSC
www.fsc.org

Contents

	Foreword by Rufus Norris	vii
	Introduction	1
1.	**About Change**	15
2.	**About Theatre**	
	Processes	41
	Unconscious Bias	55
	Art	69
	Artistic versus Admin Roles	83
	Young People	101
	Self-awareness and Self-monitoring	115
3.	**About You**	129
	Finally…	149
	Get Involved	151
	Acknowledgements	153
	About Tonic	155

Foreword by Rufus Norris

Story has always been the lens through which the human race has understood itself, and the work of the storyteller – though transient – can be seismic in the moment and profound in its historical and political impact. Those storytellers, however, have almost entirely come from just one half of humanity.

'Achieving gender equality in theatre is a no-brainer,' says Lucy Kerbel – and in this illuminating work she lays out the ethical, creative, political, commercial, social and artistic arguments for why and how the historical imbalance of voice and practice must be addressed.

Her experience and knowledge as a show-maker from the factory floor roots her insight, guidance and encouragement, making it deeply practical and un-sensational. Consequently, her informed strength is twofold: it empowers action, converting weary frustration or unfocused anger into measurable and long-lasting practice. At the same time it disempowers the denial, driven by a throng of mere details, that has stunted what should be a leading example of brilliant diversity: the theatre.

As someone who railed against the gatekeepers for much of my early career, I now find myself in the privileged but often challenging position of being one. The endless deadlines, crises, triumphs and unexpected clattering obstacles are constant distractions from a simple truth: that the gatekeepers' main responsibility is to look at why they are letting who they are letting through the gates. The work that the National Theatre have been doing with Tonic Theatre is enhancing our understanding of this with both nuance and vision.

In fact, Lucy Kerbel's work through Tonic has become increasingly pivotal in helping the entire industry, through organisations and individuals, raise its game. As she points out, we are the theatre industry; it is alive in us, and will develop or stagnate under our collective stewardship. So it is timely and invaluable that she has added to that well-researched insight with this book.

In it, she ranges across history, unconscious bias, the inevitable elitism of the freelance path, the multiple ways of taking action and responsibility, self-assessment, even the exit chat at the end of a project, and in doing so breaks down the insurmountable into a staircase of constructive progress.

For the open-minded, Lucy provides both tools and imperatives. For the sceptical – and here I include myself – she calmly and completely punctures the myths both of the theatre-maker as deep-thinking and reconstructed occupier of the moral high-ground, and of the arts as the front line of all things visionary. And she reveals, step by step, the deep-rooted self-selection that has underpinned where we find ourselves today.

This book will, I hope, have a breadth of readers – the cynic, the impartial, the supporter, the activist. She answers the cynic, informs the impartial, converts the supporter into an activist and equips them all; not in a rallying cry of anger-fuelled idealism, but in a calm, pragmatic and clear-eyed way. She talks about the 'what' coming before the 'how' – knowing exactly what you want before trying to illuminate how best to achieve it. What she herself wants is inspiringly clear, and the work of Tonic – and this excellent guide as an aspect of that – is a crucial part of how it will be achieved.

Rufus Norris is Director of the National Theatre.

Introduction

One of the things I love about theatre is that it isn't a solitary activity; it can only happen when a group of people with a range of skills work together to achieve a shared goal. Some of those people are really visible in that process; they get to take a bow at the end of the evening, or get their names on the poster. Others are behind the scenes; they may be the person who built the set or looks after the accounts. The role each member of the company plays is crucial and yet no one person can put the show on alone – without the plethora of skills, talents and interests that the people around them have, there would be no production or, at least, a poorer, less well-executed one.

When it comes to the question of how we can achieve greater gender equality in the theatre industry, I think there's a similar principle at play to how we put a show on stage. It will only happen, and happen in the best way possible, if a whole range of people are involved in its creation, and can bring their own particular talent, skill and interest to the mix.

This is a book for people who want to be part of that change, whatever their starting point is or wherever they're currently working – and regardless of their gender. It's for people who may have been thinking about and active in driving for gender equality in theatre for some time – hopefully this book will give you some further sustenance as you continue on your journey. It's for people who are taking their earliest steps – hopefully it will provide you with a way in. It's for people who may simply be intrigued by the shift they see is happening in theatre at the moment and are wondering how they might be a part of it.

What this book won't do is tell you exactly what you should be doing. It's not an instruction manual; if creating a culture shift in an industry were as straightforward as assembling a model aeroplane we'd have achieved it long ago. Instead it is intended to be a springboard from which you will – if it does its job – feel inspired and equipped to come up with your own ideas and plans for how you will contribute to the wider changes that are currently happening. That's in keeping with the approach taken by Tonic, the organisation I founded six years ago. We work across the UK theatre industry, supporting it to achieve greater gender equality in its work and workforces, but we never go into an organisation and tell the people there what they should do. I never sit down with an artistic director and tell them what they should think. Instead, Tonic's job is to provide tools, information, insights, and create the circumstances in which *they* can work out for *themselves* why imbalances exist and what they could best do to address them.

By not providing all the answers in this book, I'm not letting myself off the hook, but rather I'm suggesting that many brains and perspectives on how to move forward on this very big issue will always be better than one. Because if we are going to achieve proper change across theatre – and do it in the most joyful, imaginative, thorough and effective way possible – that will require a whole range of brains on this and a whole range of approaches to it. Besides, you know the part of theatre you inhabit the best. If you come up with your own solutions to the particular challenges that exist there, the results will be more nuanced, longer lasting and stronger.

Now is a time of hugely exciting change across our industry. The last five to ten years have – in line with a broader societal reawakening to the ongoing need for feminism – meant discussions about gender equality are being had in theatre in a way they haven't for years, and arguably on a greater scale than ever before. A swathe of new artistic directors keen to place women's art and stories at the heart of their programmes – many of them themselves women – are shifting the dial, as are individual artists driving new and invigorated ways of thinking about how the canon can be staged and by whom. A questioning has begun of how our theatre organisations are run, from the administrative to the technical to the creative to the financial, and the beginnings of a reconsidering of how pay, hours and working practices feed into the debate. All of this is hugely exciting and it's providing us with the impetus and the opportunity to re-imagine what theatre can be, as an industry, an art form, and a medium through which we converse with the public.

While all of this is thrilling and positive, there remains a long, long way to go. This book explores what those of us who want to see the green shoots of change establish into permanent features in the theatre landscape can do now, so that in another thirty years' time we're not still pointing to early indicators of progress and predicting that equality is somewhere on the horizon. This will be about capitalising on the shifts that, long-fought-for, have already been achieved, and about embedding this change properly, so that it's not a brief burst of brilliance before things return to how they have always been. It's also about ensuring we properly check that progress really *is* happening, not simply settling for the outward, and at times deceptive, signs that it is.

Having been working towards this change over the last six years, I'm firmly of the opinion that everyone who has a stake in theatre – whether they work in it, teach it, study it, watch it, or make it – has the potential and the opportunity to get involved in driving forward change. You don't have to be the Artistic Director of the National Theatre to make change happen. You can be an A-level student just embarking on a Theatre Studies course. Granted, if you are a student then there are certain things that, realistically, you can't do that the Artistic Director of the National Theatre can. But conversely there are things that *you* can do that he can't: there are ideas that you will have; there is a perspective you will bring to the subject; there is a language you are in command of that he isn't, and you can use all of these things to make your own contribution at the same time as he is making his. If many people enact many types of change on many different scales and in many different settings across theatre, a major shift will occur. Working together on the shared goal of achieving greater gender equality is like collaborating to put the most brilliant production on stage. Collectively we have a shared goal; through each contributing our own skill, knowledge and creativity, we will achieve it in the most successful manner.

About writing this book

I founded Tonic Theatre in 2011 to support the theatre industry to achieve greater gender equality in its workforces, on and off stage, and in its repertoires.

Prior to starting Tonic I worked as a freelance director for several years. During that time I was aware that, when it came to gender, there were big imbalances in the industry I worked in. I'd spotted that when I went to the theatre (and that was a lot) the casts on stage and the names of the creative teams and playwrights in the programmes were overwhelmingly male, especially when I was at the larger theatres. I had noticed that when working on a production I was often, as a woman, a minority in the rehearsal room or a tech. I was aware that the list of actors' names I'd personally worked with far outnumbered those of actresses. I saw all this and yet just got on with it; the situation was admittedly crummy but hey, that was just the way the world worked, wasn't it? I had my own career in directing to pursue and how was I ever going to get on if I allowed myself to be distracted by something that would probably sort itself out in a few years' time anyway? With the naivety of someone in their early twenties, I assumed it would all be fixed by the time I was in my thirties. Besides, we were pretty much there. Weren't we?

A working visit to Stockholm in early 2009 completely reconfigured my thinking and shattered my carefully constructed sense of inertia. While there I stumbled across the remarkable work that the Swedish performing-arts industries had been doing to improve gender equality over the preceding few years. Sure, everyone there told me that there was still far to go, but it wasn't difficult to see that their performing arts had been altered dramatically over a five or so year period. I was actually stunned. I'd been living quite happily in a deeply unequal system but telling myself in a resigned manner (and, if I'm honest, to avoid the responsibility of doing anything about it): 'That's just how it is.' Having got on a plane and flown in one direction for a couple of hours, I'd learned that is not necessarily 'how it is' nor, back in the UK, how it automatically had to be.

Sweden as a society is far ahead of ours in terms of gender equality in certain key respects. In particular, the Swedish government's focus on supporting working families and ensuring men and women have equal paternity/maternity rights and responsibilities mitigates some of the key challenges faced by theatre professionals, especially female, in the UK. But regardless of this, what was striking when I spoke to people in Sweden was how many used the term 'golden age' to describe the phase they felt their theatre industry was having. Proactively targeting gender inequalities had released a rush of talent into their field, both in terms of individual people working in the industry, and by excavating long-forgotten or previously little-known artistic works by or about women. Wow, I remember thinking, wouldn't it be wonderful to create a similar injection of energy in the UK?

I began thinking a great deal about how this could be done. Over the period of about two years I went on a self-driven journey of discovery, focused on understanding firstly why things were unequal here, and secondly how they could be made different. I started thinking about the situation a lot, and sometimes this involved bringing into the conscious part of my brain some of the instances of inequality I'd absorbed but which I assume had lodged in my unconscious; pragmatically I was aware of these inequalities on some fundamental level, but I hadn't actually processed them. I'd not inspected them, turned them over like a pebble in my hand, hadn't really examined their composition, wondered where they had come from or how they could be dispelled. I'd just accepted them as immutable. But suddenly I found myself thinking: what were the norms that had to be challenged? And what are the best forms for those acts of challenge to take?

The eventual result of this train of thought was Tonic Theatre. Tonic is an unusual theatre company in that we don't put on plays. That's because staging productions is massively time-consuming, energy-sapping and expensive (even a fringe show can now easily cost upwards of £20,000 to stage in London, where Tonic is based) and, besides, I didn't think us putting on plays would have brought Tonic any closer to achieving our ultimate goal. From the beginning, Tonic's aspiration was to create a culture shift in terms of how the theatre industry thought about and responded to gender inequalities. Us staging one or two small-scale productions a year – about all we could have afforded or managed to have done back then – wouldn't have made a dent. There had to be a better way.

At the same time, it seemed there was a moment of opportunity that hadn't necessarily been there before and I was desperate to grab it. Around this time, circa 2010, there were conversations about the situation for women in theatre bubbling to the surface that I, as someone who'd entered the industry some ten years before, hadn't heard before, or certainly not at that level of intensity or with such regularity. Questions were being asked about why things still didn't seem to be demonstratively better and why the inevitable progress women in the industry had been envisaging since the 1970s still hadn't materialised. It seemed that the subject was back on the agenda but, without a concerted effort to keep it there, could easily fall away again. If the window of opportunity was not wide open, it was at least propped slightly ajar. Getting through it and forcing it wider open – and quickly, before the industry's attention switched to something else – felt important. The mood towards change happening was, largely, open – and so a catalyst was required to speed that change up, to intensify it, solidify it, and ensure it reached as many parts of the industry and benefitted as many women, and as many types of women, as possible.

Instead of attempting to create change by leading through example – i.e. putting on plays in a gender-balanced manner and hoping the industry (which probably wouldn't even have known we existed) somehow magically followed suit – Tonic decided to offer something that at that point didn't exist: we became the first providers of a service that gave the UK theatre industry the support, information, guidance and practical assistance it needed to make progress in regards to gender equality. I began initiating conversations with theatres across the country, essentially asking them 'How can we help?' I offered Tonic as a support mechanism to enable them to better understand why imbalances existed within their work and working practices, and then expressed Tonic's desire to collaborate with them to devise and trial alternative approaches. We prioritised building relationships with those organisations that had the highest profile, and the lion's share of funding, resources and clout – the big players if you will – because we knew that if they changed how they made work, took decisions, and built their artistic programme, they would take others with them. Sometimes this work happened on a one-to-one basis with a theatre. Often, though, we concentrated on bringing together cohorts of organisations, recognising that working on a problem with a group of colleagues is often far more interesting and productive than doing it solo. Our flagship Advance programme was designed with this in mind; over a six-month period we guide a cohort of organisations through a process of research, self-reflection and group activities, enabling them to create targeted change within their own companies while considering how, collectively, they can initiate industry-wide shifts (there is lots more information on Advance at www.tonictheatre-advance.co.uk).

This approach is one that has been received with great positivity by the theatre industry. To date, our partners on such work have included major institutions such as the National Theatre, Royal Shakespeare Company, West Yorkshire Playhouse, Young Vic, Northern Stage, Chichester Festival Theatre, Sheffield Theatres, New Wolsey Theatre, the Almeida, the Tricycle, English Touring Theatre and Headlong. Demand for our work has seen us expand into opera and dance, where we've collaborated with organisations such as the Royal Opera House, Sadler's Wells and Northern Ballet. We are in the process of broadening our remit even further, into the wider creative industries, and are beginning to engage with TV and film.

Beyond supporting organisations to re-imagine their working practices, we connect them with great work that has women's voices, ideas and creativity at its heart. For instance, my 2013 book *100 Great Plays for Women* was created because I'd realised the reason so few plays with female-centric casts were being staged was a belief that, beyond *Top Girls*, few high-quality plays with mainly female casts had ever been written. In *100 Great Plays for Women*, by introducing just a hundred such works, I sought to ensure theatres could never again use a lack of available material as a reason not to depict the lives and experiences of women on stage. Similarly through Platform – a series of new scripts for young actors with mainly female casts that we commission, publish, and then disseminate to schools, colleges and youth theatres – we seek to disrupt the expectation that tomorrow's generation of theatre-makers and audience members may otherwise grow up with, about the incapacity of women to be at the centre of drama.

At just six years old Tonic is still a young organisation and I'm aware that in many ways we're still just at the start of things. And yet the level of change I have been privileged to witness first-hand during Tonic's life to date has been extraordinary. Of course, there is still far to go before theatre in this country becomes equal. But what is so heartening is the number of us from across the industry – organisations and individuals – that are committing to making this journey together. If it continues to be as fascinating as it has been to this point, I cannot wait to see where it will lead us next.

January 2017

About this book

This book is divided into three sections:

In **Part 1: About Change** we'll start by talking about change, and I'll be seeking to convince you that, while it may look like a daunting thing for an individual to achieve, it doesn't need to be. We'll look at some of the forms that change can take and will consider what the benefits of being a change-maker are.

Part 2: About Theatre is a series of provocations, designed to explode the question of why theatre remains imbalanced, while, hopefully, providing a few 'light bulb' moments for you along the way about what can be done to remedy this situation. Each provocation looks at gender inequalities in theatre from a different angle, focusing on certain aspects of how we work, think and behave which, based on what I've seen and heard over the last six years, are particularly worthy of our attention if we are to move forward as an industry. They aren't exhaustive (someone else writing this book may have selected entirely different areas of focus), aren't listed in any particular order of importance, and some may speak more directly to you than others, depending on what area of theatre you are most connected to. However, I hope all of them, even those that feel distant to your particular involvement in theatre, will be interesting to you and useful in achieving a holistic understanding of the manifold challenges we face – and the solutions available to us.

Finally, in **Part 3: About You** I'll be saying: 'Okay, now over to you', and giving you some space to think about what you want to do next. By that point you should hopefully be raring to go, but before you go tearing off on a change-making mission, we'll spend some time looking at how you can ensure that the approach you take is strategic, realistic, structured, and conducted in such a way as to stand the very best chance of being successful. We'll be looking at tools you can equip yourself with, either to embark on or develop your work, to measure your progress and also to keep you on track. Above all, we'll be focusing on how you can ensure that the change you achieve is meaningful and long-lasting.

Whatever your involvement in theatre, and whatever your engagement in the subject of gender equality has been up to this point, this is something that you can be a part of. The opportunity for us to collectively remodel, re-imagine, and refresh what our industry and our art form could be is ours for the taking. It's a mission I hope many of us will work alongside each other to achieve.

1 About Change

What is it, and how can we achieve it?

About Change

Let's begin by talking about plastic bags, bicycles, and eating lunch at your desk.

The change that you (yes, *you*) can make and do make

It may be, that having read my introduction to this book, you were left feeling 'Okay, that's all very well-intentioned but, to come back down to earth, how the hell could *I* realistically change things?' Perhaps you feel utterly disempowered in regards to your position in theatre or your ability to impact on what feels like the immoveable monolith of inequalities. Alternatively, you might be someone who *is* in a position of seniority or influence in theatre – you're absolutely the kind of person who should be driving change – and yet, when you look at your already overwhelming 'to do' list, may find yourself thinking: 'But how the hell am I going to find time to sort out gender equality on top of everything else I have to do?!'

In response to both of these quite understandable concerns I would say that you are never without agency, nor does creating change automatically have to add to your workload, but often simply entails doing things you're doing already, but in a slightly different way. To take this idea down to a really simplistic level: all of us have a choice over what we choose to watch – what we spend our money on buying tickets for and how we dedicate the time we allocate to watching theatre. We all have the power to vote with our feet and to channel our energies selectively – actively to seek out, engage in, and support work by and about women, as well as that by and about men. Granted, that may feel like a small amount of influence or altered behaviour, but if enough people do it, it sends a powerful message about the type of work audience members want to see to the theatres commissioning, selecting and producing it.

In addition, everybody, whether they are aware of it or not, automatically plays a role in determining the nature of the culture around them. By way of illustration, years ago I did an admin role in a theatre within a team of about six or seven people. At some point, probably because she was going through a busy patch, one member of the department stopped going out for lunch or spending it in the green room. Instead she'd eat a sandwich at her desk and keep working in the meantime. Without any discussion about it, gradually over the next few weeks, the rest of us in the department began regularly eating our lunch at our desks too. The person who'd done it first wasn't our boss, nor was she more senior than most people in that department and she never looked disapprovingly at anyone who wasn't eating their lunch at their desk. In fact, she probably hadn't clocked her actions were something the rest of us were even paying attention to. But very subtly her behaviour affected ours. There was a shift in the culture that she drove by changing her behaviour. By deciding that she was going to start eating her lunch at her desk, something happened to the rest of us and we began to do that too.

Obviously that example is one of negative rather than positive change – because stepping away from your desk for sixty minutes at lunchtime is probably one of the best ways of ensuring you do a good day's work – and I imagine the person who initiated the desk-eating would be dismayed to know that's what she had done. But, of course, it can work the opposite way too. Whatever space any of us finds ourselves in, whether that's a rehearsal room, or an office, or a classroom, there is a culture within that space and by dint of our physical presence there we can impact on and alter that culture. If we are a little thoughtful about how to achieve it, we can do that in a positive way.

It's also worth pointing out that a person can never be too young to affect change. In 2015 you may have read in the news about sixth-form student Jessy McCabe who, perturbed to start her A-level Music course and find not a single female composer had been included on the syllabus, successfully lobbied Edexcel, the exam board, to add a range of female composers to their specification from the following year. At the age of only seventeen, McCabe initiated a change that will alter what countless music students coming up behind her will have the opportunity to learn about the contribution that women have made to the development of Western music.

And just as someone can never be too junior to affect change, neither can anyone be too senior to make way for it. When a sixth-form student picked up on and flagged an inequality that the powers that be at Edexcel either hadn't noticed, or hadn't considered important enough to address, they had the humility and sense to recognise that the work they did – compiling a list of composers to be studied by students – could be done in a slightly different way in future so that it included women as well as men. Perhaps the articulacy of Jessy McCabe, not to mention the opinions of the four thousand people who signed her online petition, made them realise that this change to their specification was needed in order to ensure it would be relevant to and appropriate for the young people engaging with it.

We all have the capacity to create change. Sometimes the first step towards doing so is simply recognising that fact.

Small actions can create big changes

Creating change can be a full-time job. But it can also be an activity that – if done smartly – can be effective and yet not dominate your day-to-day existence. That's because sometimes putting things into place that instigate just tiny changes in the behaviour that you and the people around you exhibit can lead to impressive levels of change.

I'm writing this not long after the introduction of the plastic carrier-bag tax. In October 2015, the UK government, following the lead of other countries, made it compulsory for retailers above a certain size to charge customers a minimum of five pence per plastic carrier bag rather than giving them away for free, as the overwhelming majority had previously done. The law was designed to reduce the number of harmful plastic bags going into landfill every year and reduce the resources used in producing and transporting them. Within six months of the law being introduced, the government reported that carrier-bag use had dropped by a phenomenal 85 per cent.

I find this fascinating as an example of change in action because the shift it required of the public – shelling out five pence to receive a plastic bag rather than getting one for free – was so small and yet the impact it appears to have had within the first few months is so big. I think in many ways this isn't because of the money entailed – a five-pence coin is the sort you might lose into the lining of your purse without missing it and represents a tiny percentage of the cost of most shopping trips – but rather because it has created a mechanism whereby a moment of thought has been inserted into an everyday process where previously there wasn't one. It used to be that we would get to the front of the queue and automatically be handed or pick up a plastic bag. Since the introduction of the tax, however, an additional step has been added to that process: the cashier or self-service till now *asks* us whether we need a bag.

It's a tiny moment and yet has created a whole range of changes in how we think, feel and behave: now the onus is on us to request a bag rather than automatically receiving one. That's introduced a transactional nature to how we think about plastic bags and has changed how we view them as objects – it has flagged that there is an environmental (as well as monetary) cost to our use of them and has altered their status in the eyes of the public from seemingly benign and immaterial, to being of consequence, something further underlined by the government's interest in and imposition of a tax on them. It's possibly made the idea of wastefully using lots of them feel a bit embarrassing to us, or has given us the opportunity to feel all warm and fuzzy when we decline new bags. And it's also led to many retailers providing higher-quality carrier bags, ones that are properly reusable, rather than already torn and splitting by the time you get your shopping home.

It's worth saying that the plastic-bag tax, while positive, of course hardly begins to make a dent in regards to landfill or climate change. Until we're all thinking about how much we consume: where it was grown or produced, how it travelled to our supermarkets and high streets, how it is packaged and what its lifespan is, worrying about the bag we carry it home in is, if not immaterial, rather far from the nub of the issue. And yet the introduction of the plastic-bag tax remains an example of positive change. It has demonstrated that the public will, if the mechanism for change is right, accept and even embrace doing things differently. It is an early step, which will hopefully be followed by many more, towards making us all more responsible for the things we buy and use.

Change can seem like a daunting thing to affect, as though it needs huge power and clout and energy to be successful. But it doesn't. Sometimes it just needs something as seemingly inconsequential as the introduction of a five-pence charge – and crucially the insertion of a moment when customers pause and make a decision rather than remaining on autopilot. This is enough to make others rethink how they feel towards something so commonplace they almost don't see its significance or the level of individual agency they have in relation to it.

Marginal gains

Sometimes change can be seismic and sweeping. It happens abruptly and definitively as a result of one large event, like an earthquake or a financial crash hitting a country and changing everything in its wake. More often, though, change happens incrementally, the result of a series of motivating factors which combine to produce a bigger effect.

As we saw with plastic bags, small changes can make a big difference. Where things get really exciting is when a large number of different types of small change are simultaneously enacted, meaning that, cumulatively, an even broader shift happens. This is an approach to achieving change that's sometimes described as marginal gains. It was covered a lot in the press in regards to the success of the British Cycling team at the London 2012 Olympics. That year the squad won a greater number of medals than predicted and part of this success was attributed to the fact that the performance director, Sir David Brailsford, oversaw the implementation of an approach that functioned around the idea of marginal gains. By simultaneously making a number of very small shifts to the cyclists' behaviour before and during races, the fractional increase in speed that each of these shifts led to – perhaps a millisecond here or a millisecond there –

combined to give the cyclists an advantage of a few seconds' lead; enough to push them over the line in advance of their competitors.

How did Brailsford work out what these small shifts to behaviour should be? He spent time looking at the many reasons that the squad was not performing to its maximum capacity, both during training and when racing, even if each of these on their own would make just a marginal difference to their times. So, for instance, he found that over any period of training and competing, a number of days, not many but some, were lost when members of the team would come down with common colds or bugs. So he instructed them to become far more conscientious about washing their hands on a regular basis to minimise their chances of picking up germs and becoming ill that way. He requested all cyclists to take their own pillows in their luggage when travelling away from home for training or competitions, finding an unfamiliar pillow was among the things most likely to prevent his team getting a full and good night's sleep. He implemented a system whereby press interviews conducted track-side immediately after a race were done while the cyclist continued to pedal on a static mounted bike, thereby ensuring their muscles didn't seize up in the ten or so minutes standing around waiting for the interview to begin, something that could, just fractionally, affect their performance the next day. Individually, any one of these behavioural shifts might seem too tiny to make a real difference. But in combination with one another, and many others, they did.

If we think about the idea of incremental marginal gains in regards to gender equality in the theatre industry, there's a similar impact that could be made where a series of small and apparently inconsequential acts – when performed together by a very wide group of people – could collectively change the way that the industry works. It may be that you're massively fired up and you decide that no, the kind of change *you* want to lead is fundamental and seismic – the equivalent of an earthquake – and that's great. But equally, if you finish this book feeling that you're going to initiate the equivalent of regular hand-washing or a five-pence charge in your behaviour – and that of the people you come into contact with – that is positive and important too. And of course there's nothing to stop you following that up with some bigger and more confident steps further down the line if you find those initial ones invigorating.

The importance of taking bite-sized chunks

In mentioning some of these examples, I'm not being so naive as to suggest that gender inequalities can be remedied totally – or even markedly – by a series of small incremental shifts. What is ultimately needed is something that in scale, depth and complexity far outstrips the theatrical equivalent of taking your own pillow to a hotel with you. But the principle of focusing on small things, of being specific, and of recognising that a vast range of steps and actions are required to achieve a bigger goal, is a sound one. The business-speak way of phrasing this would be to ensure the actions we commit to are SMART: those that are Specific, Measurable, Achievable, Realistic and Time-based.

One of the things which, in my experience, I've most commonly seen preventing people who would like to make change from actually getting on and doing it, is that the scale of the problem, or indeed the sheer size of their aspiration for what they would like to achieve in its place, seems so big that they become paralysed. They simply don't know how to attack something of that scale.

But there's no reason why, because we want to achieve change, we should go about it any differently to how we get anything else done. If, for instance, we were all to spend our entire working lives focused relentlessly on the big picture of what we have to achieve – whether that's running a drama department, excelling at our A levels, or production-managing a string of shows – we'd never get anything done. We'd probably be utterly overwhelmed and so instead we spend the majority of our time focusing on the individual steps we must take to achieve our bigger goals – marking one set of essays, attending one lesson, leading one production meeting – while sporadically checking in with the bigger picture so we don't drift off track.

We do this because we recognise there's a difference between knowing *what* is important to us and identifying *how* we're going to achieve it. Imagine it's the day of an actor's opening performance in a new role. Undoubtedly they want to give a good performance. If, however, you were to ask that actor what they were going to focus on before curtain-up and they simply said 'Being good tonight', that would be rather vague and meaningless. Instead, most actors would probably break that desire to be good down into a series of discrete actions: I'm going to run through my lines during the day; I'm going to arrive at the theatre with plenty of time to spare so I'm not feeling flustered; I'm going to avoid eating anything heavy or overdosing on caffeine before the performance; I'm going to warm up fully; I'm going to take some time to focus my mind before my first entrance. These individual achievable actions should, provided the actor has taken a similarly targeted approach to rehearsals, be far better tools in carrying them several steps closer to achieving their aspiration to be good on stage than simply visualising the end result they want.

The same is true with creating change regarding gender equality in theatre. If, following similar lines to our actor example, a literary manager said their goal was to 'ensure gender equality in terms of how my theatre commissions and programmes plays', that needs to be broken down into a series of smaller, more targeted goals which, when accumulated, could get that literary manager closer to the overall super-objective they have identified. For example: I'm going to start requesting that all unsolicited scripts are submitted anonymously so I don't make assumptions based on my perceived gender of the writer; I'm going to ensure our reading panel is gender-balanced; I'm going to think about how the script meetings can be chaired by me so that the views expressed by the female readers are listened to and given as great a level of consideration as the men's; I'm going to allot time in my schedule to seek out and read more historical work by women than I have to date.

In this way, by taking one step at a time, change that can feel mind-bogglingly big to begin with can, over time, be achieved. All of us, regardless of our role or level of seniority in theatre, can pursue a thought process like this. We should give ourselves permission to see change as a string of separate, achievable actions we can pursue, rather than one single Herculean task, and then enjoy cracking on with it.

Why Bother?

Nothing I've said so far is to pretend that creating change isn't hard work. It is. Change can present itself in unpredictable ways and that in itself, when you're the one trying to manage it, can be difficult. It can be frustrating when it doesn't happen as quickly as you'd hoped or play out in the way you'd planned. Paradoxically, a step forward can sometimes lead to a step backwards because the signs of progress can trick us into thinking a problem is solved and so it gets forgotten about and reverts to form. Some people can feel unsettled, or affronted, or insecure when confronted with change, and dealing with the negative responses of those around you because you are attempting to create positive shifts can be demoralising, angering, even upsetting. And so, in light of all this, being really clear about why change is important enough to you to bother pursuing it is crucial.

The importance of identifying why change is important to *you*

In the face of what isn't necessarily a straightforward or easy activity to take part in, a really useful first step (or indeed a really useful step along the way, when you've been at it for a while but find yourself flagging) can be to ask yourself – or remind yourself – why do you want to create change? Why is it important to you? And important enough to make it worth the effort? In short: why bother?

A quick task for you: grab a pen and paper and give yourself exactly two minutes to write (time yourself). Try to write non-stop – don't stop to think or censor yourself or try to craft what you're saying. Just write down what comes into your mind spontaneously in response to the following question:

Why is gender equality in theatre important to me?

After you've done that, take a couple of moments to read back over what you've written and simply give yourself time to clock anything that surprises you or jumps out as particularly inter-esting or important in what you've just written. Maybe underline or draw a circle around any key words or ideas. They may be useful for you to refer to later.

Taking time to either locate for yourself – or rearticulate to your-self – why this subject is important to you, and what it is that you care about in relation to it, is crucial. That's because, generally, the impetus behind anyone trying to change anything is that they care about it in some way. So asking myself why I care enough to put myself through the hassle of trying to create change in theatre is something I do every so often. It keeps me on track and reminds me why I'm bothering. It also connects me back to the core of why *I* am doing all this – what is it about this that matters to *me*? Why do *I* care? And also, perhaps selfishly (although if selfishness is a motivating factor in me driving for positive change, that's fine by me), what's in it for *me*?

If change is going to happen, it's down to us

Only individual human beings can create change. Yes, there are theatres, and companies, and organisations, and institutions, and unions that populate our industry and they must get behind change for it to happen in its fullest sense. But any one of these is only ever made up of a group of individuals. I've seen phenomenal positive shifts being enacted by individuals: directors, artistic directors, writers, technicians, educators, administrators, actors, just because they decided they would. Some of these people had access to significant funds and profile. Others didn't. Some have been publically celebrated. Others haven't. But all of them got engaged in some way; emotionally, politically, creatively or intellectually in the question of why we're still not equal – and responded to it in considered, intelligent and innovative ways. They have delivered change while taking our industry just a step closer to what they would like it to be.

None of us are tenants of someone else's industry; we *are* theatre and if we don't change it to be what we dream it could be, no one else will. We're not going to get given permission to change it because there is no one who's in a position to grant that permission. If we want to create change, the only people we have to ask permission of are *ourselves*.

Why Wouldn't You Bother?!

So yes, change is hard to achieve. It requires grit, determination, patience and sometimes courage. And yet the rewards, for those who engage in making it happen, can be huge.

Creating change – what's in it for you?

Some of the rewards of creating change are personal; they directly impact in a positive way on the person who is bothering to go to the effort of doing the change-making work, a bit like the fact that bothering to go for a run every morning will, over time, benefit your physical and mental well-being, despite the outlay of energy and time that is required. As I previously mentioned, I sometimes ask myself the question 'What's in it for me?' when, especially on the days it feels difficult, I find myself wondering why I should persist in trying to achieve change in theatre. There are many answers to this, but among the primary ones that's consistently towards the top of my list is that – on a personal level – I find change absolutely fascinating; even when it's hard I hugely enjoy the process of trying to drive change. I find it an incredibly stimulating and creative thing to do.

If I were to try to analyse why this is, I'd say it's because change is inherently dramatic. It's what, when I was directing, I spent most days in the rehearsal room exploring with actors.

Essentially, most drama is about change: characters trying to affect change, or going through a process of change, either in themselves or witnessing it in the world around them. If you get to the end of watching a play and nothing and no one on stage has changed, you can bet it wasn't a particularly dramatic piece of work. The thing I most loved about being a director was spending time excavating the script, trying to work out what the change was that the characters wanted to affect on a moment-by-moment basis and then, with the actors, exploring the various tactics those characters could use to achieve this.

Today, I'm seldom found in a rehearsal room, but that fascination I feel towards the nature of change, and which I'm trying to achieve with Tonic, has, I think, its roots there. But that's just me. For someone else, the thing that gets them hooked on change-making will be that they are instinctive storytellers and have stories they're burning to tell on stage. For others it may be about the crossover between their personal politics and the way they want to express themselves artistically, or experience their workplace. For someone else it may be their desire to ensure the company, or team, or department they are part of runs as successfully and effectively as it can.

Change-making as a tool for personal empowerment

Regardless of the initial impetus, one of the biggest benefits, as far as I'm concerned, to *anyone* involved in making change is that it is empowering to do. And in an industry that can, inadvertently or otherwise, leave many of its members feeling without agency quite a lot of the time, finding empowerment is no small thing. The knowledge that you've succeeded in leaving somewhere or something just a little bit better than when you found it is never going to make a person feel anything other than good about themselves. Whether that's making sure your college's library now has a wide stock of plays by women on its shelves as well as a wide stock of plays by men, or using your influence to ensure the culture in the rehearsal room you're part of is one that is respectful and welcoming to all, making things better is one of the simplest but best approaches we can all take to be happy in what we're doing.

Of course, the more major the change you're driving, the more positive the affirmation will be, especially when you reach a point where you realise you are playing a role in changing what theatre looks like and broadening our conception of what it can be and do. Let's take as an example the strides that have been taken by key individuals regarding cross-gender casting in Shakespeare in the UK in the last few years. It's a practice with a long history, from Sarah Bernhardt playing Hamlet to Fiona Shaw as Richard II and, outside the commercial mainstream theatre, queer theatre has consistently examined and exploded the real or perceived links between the gender of characters and the bodies that perform them. But more recently, cross-gender casting has become not only more prevalent, but more pervasive and pointed, used to comment on inequalities in our world and restore a sense of balance in our industry. It has also given us new lenses through which we can reconsider our treasured narratives, those that, rightly or wrongly, remain at the heart of our dramatic heritage and so greatly influence our theatrical identity.

To select just one of many recent breakthroughs, the Donmar Warehouse's 2012 all-female production of *Julius Caesar*, produced in collaboration with Clean Break and with director Phyllida Lloyd and actress Harriet Walter at the helm, felt like something of a landmark production. That wasn't because all-female Shakespeare hadn't happened before in the UK, but rather because it hadn't quite happened at that scale, with that level of profile or, in terms of the aesthetic behind the production, arguably with that level of directness in terms of what, politically, it was saying. That staging of *Julius Caesar*, by a group of women, on a stage in the West End of London, was in and of itself an act of change-making. It marked the first time that a group of women had gotten their hands on a set of tools – that play, those roles, that stage, that level of resourcing – that up until then, and in that combination, only men had enjoyed. Just imagine how that group of actresses taking their curtain call after their first performance of *Julius Caesar* must have felt, or the technical, creative or production staff in the audience or the wings, who had each played a role in ensuring that production got on to that stage. Absolutely electric, I would imagine. Not only had they made history, but they had succeeding in shouldering open a door which, certainly as far as cross-gender casting in the classics has gone since then, has made it significantly easier for others to pass through and, therefore, move the practice even further forward.

There's something brilliant in not just changing something, but changing it to be a bit more like you believe it ought to be, especially if your vision is of creating something that is fairer, more interesting, and more embracing of difference.

Theatre shouldn't be untouchable, nor should we regard its practices as hallowed; like any other industry it isn't perfect and we have the right to question, challenge and develop it. And we don't need to treat it with kid gloves. Theatre isn't going to break; it's tough – it's survived in just about every time, culture and society, and can be bent and stretched in endless directions yet lose none of its potency or appeal. So if we don't like it, we can change it. A healthy dose of skepticism about why we do what we do, a pinch of irreverence, and a twist of subversion are no bad things with which to equip ourselves when considering where we want to take our theatre industry next.

The Wider Benefits of Creating Positive Change

If I've failed to sell change-making to you on the personal benefits alone, let's take some time to look at the broader benefits – to our industry, our art form, and also, crucially, to our audiences. Because finding ways to make theatre more equitable for men and women isn't just something that will be good for women. It will be good for everyone. In fact, I'd go so far as to say that achieving gender equality in theatre is a no-brainer; if we can work out how to take advantage of the full pool of talent available to us, rather than just parts of it, we will create a broader, richer palette of work for our audiences, and we will run our organisations and structures in a more effective and successful way.

Greater diversity = greater success

Let's start first with the point about running our organisations and structures more effectively. Countless studies conducted across all sorts of industries and workplaces have demonstrated time and time again that having a range of experiences, perspectives and skills represented across any group of people – whether that group is a small team, a department or an entire company – will make that group higher functioning and more successful. This stands to reason. If you have a diverse range of people coming at a shared problem from multiple different starting places, their collective response will be more imaginative, complex and – most likely – successful, because between them they will be able to suggest a multiplicity of approaches based on the wide base of experience they collectively represent. So in a theatrical context, whether that 'shared problem' is 'What shall we programme on our stages next season?' or 'How can we best design our brochure to attract the public to see our work?', or 'How might we translate *Hamlet* from 200 pages of written text into a three-dimensional live performance?', having a range of people – not just of different genders but also a mix of ages, ethnicities, socio-economic backgrounds, educational backgrounds, geographical locations, and so on – will be far more likely to elicit imaginative decision-making. It also helps protect against decisions being made with little or no scrutiny: the 'but that's just how people like us get stuff done' approach, which it is so easy for any homogenous group to employ, whether they realise it or not.

Here's a specific example: imagine a theatre has a front-of-house team in which no one on that team has a disability, or experience of regularly attending public events with someone who has a disability, or any kind of training in delivering the best customer experience for people with disabilities. There is an increased chance that the team won't be as high functioning as it could be in regards to offering a good service to disabled patrons (or, it could be argued, any patrons). There will inevitably be things that they will miss; opportunities they won't spot, problems they won't identify, and solutions they will struggle to arrive at, which may mean that a proportion of potentially loyal audience members either don't come to that theatre in the first place or, if they do, feel less than enthusiastic about returning. And when approximately one in five adults in the UK has a disability, that's a large chunk of your potential audience to remain unresponsive to. If the composition or experiences of that front-of-house team were more reflective of that of the general public, the team would collectively stand a better chance of doing its job as successfully as it possibly could.

Making the commercial case

This particular example segues nicely into another argument for greater equality in theatre: the commercial case. For some people working in theatre, particularly on the commercial side (i.e. those in the West End whose work is not subsidised by Arts Council or other public funds), their predominant responsibility is safeguarding the financial health of their organisation because, put simply, if they fail to attract investors or turn a profit they cease to be able to make theatre. Often the case for equality and diversity in theatre is made from the ethical perspective; that it's right and fair that all sorts of people should have access to making theatre and see themselves reflected there. And of course that's proper and correct, and it's important we continue to discuss the subject on these terms. But there's also a very sound commercial case to be made and, if it compels some people to drive or make way for change on that basis, we should take advantage of that.

A couple of years ago I was invited to speak about equality and diversity at a film festival in New York, and one of the people appearing on the same panel as me was a highly dynamic Vice President of one of the major entertainment corporations in the US. Her particular remit is to increase diversity across the output of the corporation, and one of the things she spoke about was a recent TV drama the corporation had produced which was unusual among its drama output in that the cast was not predominantly white, but almost entirely African American or mixed race. The show had been an outstanding commercial success and a mainstream critical hit. It was one of the corporation's recent big success stories. The conversation she said she'd been having with her colleagues when arguing for the commissioning of the series (and a whole range of other work that better reflects America's diversity) was that the public in the US no longer looks like the one that the TV networks have been depicting on screen. By being at the forefront of producing prime-time drama about people who rarely see themselves represented on screen – and yet make up a significant (and growing) proportion of the country's population and TV audience – the corporation had the chance to seize a market. Making the business case to those people whose primary responsibility and focus is on keeping the books balanced, can be among the most successful ways to instigate change.

Making the artistic case

Beyond the commercial argument there is, of course, the artistic case to be made for gender equality. That's to say that by enabling a greater number of women, and a greater number of women who possess a wide range of characteristics or who represent a broad range of backgrounds and experiences, to reach their potential as artists and to receive a platform for their work, we will open up our stages to a richer, more diverse variety of stories, and ways of telling stories. That may be because more stories written by, or about, women are being made available to audiences and presented on equal terms to those written by or about men. But also because more women are given the opportunity to push the boundaries of how theatre can be constructed, whether through how a show is directed, or designed, its music composed, fight scenes choreographed, or the way in which its characters are embodied and scenes performed. Giving a wider range of theatre-makers the opportunity to speak directly to audiences will ensure a wider range of *ways* of speaking to audiences are uncovered and developed. And this is exciting for all of us.

Making the social case

Finally, and this is the one that personally gets me going the most, there is the social case for achieving greater gender equality in theatre. Theatre acts as a mirror to society, and those of us who make it, programme it, teach it and promote it have a responsibility to do that accurately – not to cut large chunks of the population out of the picture. Creating theatre – whether that's putting on a show in the biggest theatre in the West End or staging an amateur performance in a village hall – is a privilege because it provides those of us that do it with a platform. It's a platform from which we get the undivided attention of a captive audience night after night, something most political parties and corporate marketing departments would kill for. Certainly today the theatre is not as political and persuasive a platform as it once was. It's not anywhere near as big as the platforms provided by TV, film or the media. But it is a platform none the less. Platforms are all around us, but if when a person looks to those platforms – to the stages, screens and billboards around them – and does not see themselves represented there, I think that does something to a person. Worse still, if, on the occasions they *do* see themselves depicted, it is in a way that is consistently demeaning, or undermining, or inauthentic, or critical, that does something to them again, and that thing is not a good thing.

Theatre gives us the opportunity to change how people feel about themselves and others. If we use this privilege in a positive way, to give equal voice and profile to women (and all sorts of women) as well as men, we will be making our own contribution towards challenging the imbalances that persist across our society, rather than reaffirming or compounding them.

All in all, making change happen has masses of positives: it's interesting, empowering, makes you feel good about yourself, and – to the benefit of all – makes theatre a better place to be and a more interesting art form to experience.

But Remember... Before You Can Change the World You First Have to Understand It

I often find myself saying, particularly to students and young people I come into contact with: before you can change what you don't like about anything – whether that's theatre or the wider world – you first need to understand why it is as it is. That's because to subvert a norm successfully, you not only need to have identified what that norm is, but, crucially, what has led to its existence. Otherwise, when you're trying to change it, you're not going to know where to begin, nor the specifics of what you're combating.

This is why Tonic, in its desire to drive change, has always taken a knowledge-based approach. We do lots of research before trying to address any problem in an effort to best understand why it is as it is. This is how we describe what we do on our website:

> Tonic's approach involves getting to grips with the principles that lie beneath how our industry functions – our working methods, decision-making processes and organisational structures – and identifying how, in their current form, these can create barriers. Once we have done that, we devise practical yet imaginative alternative approaches and work with our partners to trial and deliver them. Essentially, our goal is to equip our colleagues in UK theatre with the tools they need to ensure a greater level of female talent is able to rise to the top.

Tonic has never considered itself a campaigning organisation (although I would say that advocacy is certainly part of our remit, as is raising awareness of imbalances that exist) because our predominant focus is not on simply pointing out that a problem exists, but rather on designing and implementing solutions whereby the problem can be fixed. We don't engage in calling people out or 'naming and shaming', nor do we dedicate our time to telling theatres what they should look like, but instead on helping them to achieve the necessary change. I appreciate the importance of those organisations that do operate in this manner, and recognise the tireless campaigning conducted by individual women and women's theatre groups over the last few decades that has provided the foundations upon which Tonic and many other organisations and individuals are able to do the equality-focused work we are doing today. But that wasn't the style of change-making that I wanted to do when I first founded Tonic, nor does it hold any appeal to me today. I didn't want to be on the outside, pointing a finger at what, from a distance, seemed to be wrong. It was far more interesting to me to be on the inside, collaborating with others to fix it.

To solve a problem, it's first crucial to have a clear understanding of what the causes of it are and what, up until now, has prevented it getting better. I'd say that over the last six years of my work with Tonic I've pretty rarely found that out-and-out misogyny is the cause for imbalances. Almost always it was a far more complex and subtle range of barriers systemically created and reaffirmed by the manner in which theatre has evolved to think, behave and operate, influenced, of course, by inequalities between men and women in the wider world. Without knowledge of the nature of the problem, if you go crashing into a situation not fully appreciating why it is as it is, there's a risk you could fail to identify key opportunities or levers that could help you create change. Or you may misfire your ammunition, directing your energy or resources towards targets that are never going to yield results. In extreme examples, you could risk making a situation even worse, perhaps because your ignorance gets the backs up of the very people you most need to enlist and win the trust of, thereby making them even more rigid in their behaviour.

Tooling yourself up with knowledge is a crucial step when trying to achieve change. In the next section of this book I'll be attempting to give you a précis of some of the insights and information I've gained, or others have shared with me, into what the barriers are to equality, and some of the key areas that we could, most profitably, turn our attention to as an industry. It's not exhaustive. But it should hopefully offer a way in for those of you who are newer to the subject, while providing further food for thought for those of you who have been engaged in this for some time.

At times I zoom right out to look at the big picture, focusing on topics such as how we view art, and how we run our working practices in theatre. It's when taking this broad look that I think things get most interesting but also, potentially, most likely to feel overwhelming. But stick with it, and on the other side – in Part 3 – we'll take it back to the practical steps that you, and others around you, can take to achieve change.

2 About Theatre

Why is it imbalanced, and how can we change that?

Processes

Before we talk about theatre, and how we can achieve change in regards to gender equality, let's briefly go to a wide-angle shot. Because creating change in theatre is only possible when we consider the backdrop against which we're operating: the entire landscape, not only those conditions specific to our industry and art form.

To put it bluntly, and to get things in perspective, we're swimming against the tide of a few thousand-odd years of human history, during which the ideas, creativity, intellectualism and identity of women have overwhelmingly been ignored, suppressed, denied or undermined. In which female achievement has generally been attributed to men, if recognised at all, and the majority of people without a Y chromosome have in some way either covertly or overtly been made servile to those who have. It's a grotesque and appalling situation written like an indelible stain across our collective history. It remains the norm in significant parts of the world. There's nothing to say it won't become so again here.

When looked at through this lens, and given that theatre is a reflection of the world around us, it's little wonder that the industry is also frequently unequal.

There are two things I think it's worth pausing a moment here to clock. The first is the extreme depth and scale of the gender inequalities that have until really very recently been the unchallenged norm in our society. They have characterised who we are, and their roots are found deep in the very bedrock upon which our society is built: work, family, faith, commerce, politics, civic identity. Consequently, the actions required if change is to be achieved (and not just achieved, but sustained) are unlikely to be snappy or simple ones; essentially what is required is a fundamental rethink of how our society functions.

The second is that the size of the change required will take significant time and ongoing efforts to achieve, even if we're only talking about changing things on the micro level of the theatre industry. In many ways I think the challenge for those of us who want to make progress for women in theatre will not be whether we can come up with the ideas for creating change (theatre is, after all, teeming with intelligent, creative thinkers), but instead whether we collectively have the tenacity, stamina and enduring focus required to make these ideas successful in the face of innumerable barriers, institutional obstacles and seemingly slow progress. We'll need to apply action in a consistent manner over the long term and, crucially, not mistake an early demonstration of the *potential* for women to be better represented in theatre as the *achievement* of that actually happening. We must not mistake concentrated efforts alone, or the early signs of progress, as progress itself.

To provide an analogy: a talent scout doesn't spot a promising young athlete at a local meet, and think 'That kid has the potential to be an Olympic gold medalist' – only to walk away and be surprised that, some fifteen years later, that young person has never been heard of again. Instead, if they want to achieve success, they would need to develop that athlete over a period of years, working with them in a sustained manner through a whole programme of training and competing, a programme which – to stand a chance of being successful – must be consistent, strategic and dedicated.

The same goes for achieving greater gender equality in theatre: the potential for making it happen is evidently there, but will only be achieved if we work at it unceasingly and consistently. While there will be some brilliant, gratifying 'quick wins' along the way, this is about playing the long game and accepting that what we're working on here is a gradual but consistent cross-fade from one state to another, not a snap-change.

How we think about time

Straight away, this flags up an area we need to consider if we're going to be successful in this: how those of us involved in theatre think about time and, specifically, the time frames we allocate ourselves in which to get stuff done. In theatre, our time spans tend to be short; we often focus on relatively brief blocks of time, largely because theatre is such a deadline-driven world in which the schedule is inevitably dictated by the run-up to opening nights. So we often think about the few weeks of a rehearsal period, the few months of a season of work, or the few years of a grant period or business plan. Or if we're in an academic context, our thinking can be similarly fragmented, broken down into individual modules, terms, years, or cohorts of students. This short-termism – even if entirely necessary for getting the most pressing tasks done and ensuring the curtain goes up on time or the students graduate when they're meant to – makes conducting long-term work such as landscape change incredibly difficult. It may require twenty to forty years to be successful, rather than twenty to forty months.

So in our efforts to achieve greater gender equality, part of what we can usefully consider is how we can develop longer-term ways of working and thinking. Less blasting something in a microwave on full power for a few seconds, and more leaving it to heat through gradually in a slow cooker, so that we get as good at working over more extended periods – when seeking to create fundamental change – as we are at working in short bursts. Central to this will be us figuring out how we can sustain ourselves over this time – not get disheartened, run out of resources, energy or drive while change is taking time to 'cook'. We'll also need to think about how, in an industry often addicted to adrenaline, the rush of fast-approaching deadlines and the immediate signifiers of success, we can draw enough attention to something that doesn't need to be sorted by the end of the day. We need to get it on to people's agendas and once it's there, keep it there.

Identifying the kind of change we want to achieve

Beyond being aware of the time we will need to put into this, it's also worth asking ourselves what *kind* of change we want to achieve. For my money, the goal shouldn't be that the industry keeps going as it always has, just with a few more female faces present. Rather, I'd suggest, it's much bigger than this. It's about re-imagining how our industry works, thinks, and behaves so that it is properly inclusive of all sorts of people. I'm writing this book with a predominant focus on women, but you don't need to look far to see that theatre, or at least many areas of theatre, remain far from reflective of the population of this country in many respects: race, ethnicity, disability, sexuality, age, socio-economic background and a whole other spectrum of characteristics. Genuine change in theatre will only come once we've become genuinely inclusive of and responsive to *all* talented individuals and are telling stories about the *full* range of people who make up our society. And in order to do that, we're going to need to alter our systems.

Before I began my work with Tonic I'd always just assumed that the people who got to work in the biggest or highest-profile theatres; who had their plays staged there, got to direct, design or act in their productions, or led them as organisations were automatically the most talented, capable or exciting artistically. And of course some of them were. But when I looked again at the demographic of who was taking the majority of those jobs, things simply didn't stack up: white, able-bodied men aren't somehow biologically better programmed to make theatre than any other group. And yet the strike rate on who – when I looked around me back then – was getting the top jobs would suggest they were. So, I was forced to conclude, something in the *system* we were using to develop, nurture, process and promote some people to the exclusion of others wasn't working. It seemed to be disproportionately favouring men who happened also to be white, able-bodied (and generally middle-class) while disproportionately working against anyone who, well, wasn't.

This led me to believe that it is the system itself that needs to change. Not women. If we don't believe one group is biologically *better* engineered to make theatre, we also can't believe one group is engineered to be biologically *worse* at it. And once you've asserted that one group isn't on the whole incompetent or inept, their absence from certain parts of an industry, especially the best-funded or highest-profile bits, becomes indefensible. Given that females form the majority of students of drama and theatre studies, it isn't like women aren't interested in theatre as an art form or a career in the first place. Plus there is clearly no lack of women buying tickets and attending theatre, nor of work being made by or about women – it's just that much of it hits a bottle-neck on the fringe or in the smaller and less well-resourced spaces.

It isn't women who need support to be better writers, actors, directors, leaders or creators. Rather, it is the structure in which they operate that needs to improve to bend *to* them and their talent.

The numbers are important, but they don't tell it all

It goes without saying that taking an interest in the structures around which our industry operates doesn't preclude paying attention to the numbers. An increasing proportion of theatres are making 50:50 commitments in terms of the writers, directors and actors they work with, something I consider to be very positive. Making numerically based pledges like this and gathering empirical data on how many women compared to men get employed (and not just employed but in what fields and with what levels of resourcing) is probably one of the fastest and easiest ways of us measuring whether we are making progress or just assuming we are.

But the figures don't tell the full story, nor are numbers the only prize we should be keeping our eye on. They are just one part of a much bigger picture. This work goes further than just increasing the numbers of women to be found in specific areas or levels of the industry. It is about us being progressive in regards to how theatre functions, thinks and behaves. This is so that it is an environment in which women are not merely fitting themselves – sometimes at the expense of feeling like a square peg in a round hole – into structures which, having originally been conceived to support and meet the needs of men, don't always enable them to do their best work. Nor to be as happy as they might be in their professional lives, or reach their potential.

As an industry the indicator of our profound progress will be when we stop thinking only about *how many* women (or people of any underrepresented group) are present within any context, but when we have redesigned those structures so they are built by everyone, for everyone.

Re-imagining Our Processes in Order to Create Change

So how do we go about achieving all this? Probably the first step is recognising that we need to start doing things differently if we want to achieve gender equality. As the old saying goes: 'If you always do what you've always done, you'll always get what you've always had.' A useful starting point for this will be us thinking about how we can better evaluate and understand the impact of the processes we use.

Processes

All of us have processes, or ways of doing things, that we use again and again, ways we have 'always done things'. For instance, a theatre will have processes in place for how it techs a show, commissions a playwright, recruits for a vacancy on its staff, or programmes a season of work. Yes, there may be some variations built into these processes: a big, complex Christmas show will probably get a longer tech period than a smaller studio show; the recruitment of a staff member at executive level may see an organisation bring in a head hunter rather than simply advertising the post. But essentially those processes remain set, functioning around a series of pre-decided templates, time spans, rhythms and protocols. Likewise, an amateur dramatic or university drama society will have processes in place around how its committee makes choices about which shows to stage in any year, how some members are selected over others to perform and direct, and how funds are allocated between various productions.

Although less formal, individuals involved in theatre will often have their own processes too; as a director I know I've tended to follow a set structure when casting for plays, or approaching a script during rehearsals, and even in regards to making decisions about what plays I would and wouldn't choose to attend as an audience member.

These processes or preset ways of doing things can feel comfortable, reassuring, supportive, and sometimes, given how busy most people in theatre tend to be, vital in ensuring we get stuff done. But if we want to reconfigure our theatre industry so that we stand a chance of achieving equality, we may have to question whether these processes – the ways in which we currently do, think and work – are the key challenges we're up against. Because until we change our processes, our outputs will always remain the same.

Imagine we run a biscuit factory. It's a well-established and successful family business that's been going for generations. All our production lines are geared up to make chocolate bourbons, and very fine chocolate bourbons they are too. Say we decide our biscuit factory should change its output, so actually we're now producing a mixture of chocolate bourbons and fig rolls. The only way we're going to get those fig rolls is if we change the way the production lines function. Because if every step of our factory's processes are set up to ensure that what drops off the production line into boxes destined for the shops is a steady stream of chocolate bourbons, no amount of wishing is going to get us our fig rolls.

Often, and I'll shortly outline a few reasons for why I think this can be the case, the theatre industry tends to be poor at analysing and questioning its own processes or 'production lines'. Hand in hand with this, and possibly because the outcomes of the work we do are intrinsically so very public, there can be an over-attentiveness to output (lots of staring at boxes of chocolate bourbons, scratching our heads and wringing our hands over the persistent lack of fig rolls). What this means is that a common mistake when wanting to make change is to focus all of that effort on the point of output. This is instead of looking step by step at the 'production line' and what led to the homogeneity of the output, or trying to ascertain at what point particular barriers to certain groups of people presented themselves, or common points of drop-off occurred. Then, through this, identifying which components of the production line need to be either tinkered with or entirely redesigned to ensure that the output changes.

Let's say that a theatre company is in the latter stages of assembling its new season of work and, comparatively late in the day, the leadership team spots that the creative teams it's proposing to employ across that season are exclusively male and white. Their response at that point, not wanting to present an all-white and all-male line-up, may be quietly to swap one or two creatives out, and replace them instead with people who aren't white men. On one level, the fact the company has spotted the lack of diversity among the people it's considering employing is positive and it's arguably better that they've tried to patch it up at the eleventh hour than not at all (so long, of course, as they've not reneged on agreements already made).

However, until the company takes steps to understand *why* no women or people of colour had been considered for its line-up in the first place, come the next season the company may be in the same situation again, and the season after that, and the season after that. Because rather than understanding the cause of the problem, the company has merely tried to treat the symptom. It's also now got some creatives in the season who have been brought in in a bit of a rush and who might have a sneaking suspicion they're there to plug the diversity gap, not because the company is desperate to work with them. If the company had taken time to look at the steps along the 'production line' of how they develop relationships with freelance creatives, from the point of initial contact through to deciding to give them a job, then they would have been in a much better position to have a healthy mix of creatives.

Reviewing and re-imagining the processes you use to get stuff done can be a deeply creative and often quite liberating activity. A bit like rearranging the layout of your kitchen and realising you have more space that you realised and a design that is far more conducive to cooking. But doing, even *getting round* to doing work of this nature is not without challenge.

The challenge of busyness

Someone a while back told me about a cartoon he'd seen in which a couple of cavemen are arduously pushing a wheelbarrow full of rocks up a hill. Their task is made all the more difficult by the fact the wheelbarrow has a square wheel. At the side of the picture, a third caveman is proffering a round wheel. 'Can't stop now,' the first of the cavemen calls over his shoulder, 'we're too busy.'

This cartoon accurately sums up the major challenge the theatre industry faces (and, of course, many other industries and professions too – because theatre is not alone in being an environment where there's generally more work to do than hours in the day) in terms of updating our working processes so they are more equitable. The reality of working in most theatre organisations or drama departments in the UK is to be on an endless treadmill of extreme busyness. Deadlines are endless and, because of the nature of what we do, missing one or failing to complete a task to a decent level is a very public failure. Often all this work is being done by people with highly limited resources, surrounded by others who, like them, have workloads that feel impossibly big.

What this can mean is that, like the cavemen who are too busy to notice how much more successful they'd be in doing their job if they took the time to replace the square wheel on their wheelbarrow with a round one, we keep going with ways of working because we know they're *good enough*. They may not be great, but they just about get the job done and sometimes when we're on a treadmill of activity – or have a wheelbarrow of rocks that has to be moved from one place to another, no matter how tight the deadline – we plough on rather than stopping, assessing, and possibly redesigning. To do so can, in the short term at least, feel like an impossibility, even if in the long term it could make everyone's lives much better.

Achieving the change we want to see is about us all shifting priorities; about making a concerted effort to find the time to consider how our processes could run more successfully, to make space to discuss this where it hasn't previously been in a schedule or on an agenda, to incorporate it as a specific aspect of someone's job description or list of responsibilities so it no longer falls between the gaps. Because unless a definitive move is made to set aside the resource for this work to happen, it will constantly slip by the by.

One of the most straightforward ways I ever heard someone talk about this was a member of the senior-management team of a theatre with whom Tonic was working. After listening to a lengthy conversation among her counterparts about the ins and outs of the various challenges to them doing this work, she simply said, 'Maybe we just have to do it. Like we have to balance our budgets – and we all manage to do that – this needs to be the same; non-negotiable.' I would agree with her. It is this work in understanding what underpins everything we do in theatre and then getting that underlying structure right that is crucial. It's about making space for understanding the bigger picture, rather than simply repeating the same imperfect actions again and again because we're too busy and distracted to stop.

The importance – and necessity – of taking this step by step

Redesigning working practices might sound like a massive project in which a busy organisation or an individual should engage, but it doesn't have to be as daunting as it may sound. The young athlete's journey from promising youth to Olympian is one that can only be achieved through a series of cumulative but manageable steps of progress over the course of years, not all at once in one giant leap forward. An expert coach knows what to prioritise when developing the athlete's technique and what will naturally follow on from what, within a well-constructed programme of training which interweaves different strands over time: technique, fitness, strength, stamina, mental focus. So it is with any of us embarking on developing, strengthening and, yes, occasionally jettisoning aspects of our current working processes. It takes time and small steps towards the ultimate goal.

There's no need for us to tear the whole structure down and start again from scratch, but rather to work methodically step by step through the different elements of what we do. That could, for example, mean a theatre company questioning how it builds relationships with creatives, and then setting itself the task of appraising that over a twelve-month period. Following this, they might spend six months focusing on how they read and process scripts that are submitted, before moving on to think about the visiting work they programme for another predetermined period of time. Or this could be a youth theatre considering how, every term in an academic year, it could introduce its young people to the technical side of putting on shows through one-off workshops on areas like lighting, video, sound and stage management and then – if this sparks interest – provide structured opportunities in future productions for the young people to get involved in the technical delivery of the shows, rather than only performing in them.

Not everything has to be done at once. But my bet is that for anyone, or any organisation, that does decide to engage in this kind of work, once they get interested in the mechanics of one part of what they do, they won't be able to help but become intrigued by the rest. And then change will begin to happen before we even realise it.

Unconscious Bias

Unconscious bias may or may not be a term you're familiar with. I'm going to explain what it is for those of you who have not previously come across it and for those of you who have, treat this as a refresher. I wanted to dedicate a section of this book to this subject because, while it doesn't hold all the answers to the ongoing underrepresentation of all sorts of groups, including women, in certain key areas of theatre, it is a significant part of the picture. Unconscious bias is perhaps the one thing, above all else, that – when Tonic has delivered training on it to people – has made them go 'Aaaah, I see', and you can tell from their faces that somewhere a rather crucial penny has dropped.

What is 'unconscious bias'?

Essentially, unconscious bias refers to the short cuts our brains make when helping us to make sense of a situation or an interaction. Generally speaking, the human brain is using short cuts the whole time. These short cuts enable the brain to cut through the overload of information and stimuli presented to us every second of our waking lives so we can both survive and function. In a split second they can prevent us from making bad choices, like sticking our hand into an open flame, or can help us make good ones, like jumping out of the way of a swerving car. Put simply, these short cuts protect us.

This works not only in emergency or life-and-death situations. To a greater or lesser extent, our brains are powering away the whole time using a series of short cuts designed, if not to keep us alive, at least to make our existences highly functional. There's so much going on around us the whole time, these short cuts allow us to make decisions when faced with a potentially mind-boggling array of possiblilites. Without realising it, we rely on them to help us make good decisions over bad ones, moment by moment.

Our unconscious minds work faster than our conscious ones. A group of scientists ran a test where they gave a series of volunteers four decks of cards, two of which had red backs and two of which had blue. The volunteers were asked to select a succession of cards and it was up to them whether they chose to draw from the red packs or the blue packs. The game was about gambling money; some of the cards if selected meant the volunteer would win an amount of cash. Others if drawn meant they lost money. The scientists had weighted the cards so that a far greater proportion of the blue cards were either winning ones or, if losing ones, incurred a relatively low penalty. In contrast, more of the 'danger you're going to lose some money' cards had red backs and generally led to bigger losses. After around eighty draws of the cards, most volunteers had worked out that the more blue cards they drew, the more positive outcomes they would get and so they began to prefer selecting these over the reds. Their conscious minds had worked out the decision that would be most likely to benefit them and protect them from the danger of drawing a badly losing card.

What was interesting was that the scientists had wired up the volunteers so they could test the activity in their sweat glands under the skin on the palms of their hands, somewhere stress is readable. It's not surprising that in a gambling game – where money was at risk – volunteers showed signs of stress. But what was noticeable from an unconscious bias perspective, was how stress was more readable when volunteers reached for a red card, and this kicked in after just ten or so draws from the decks. Very early on, and before their conscious minds followed suit some seventy draws later, their unconscious minds had worked quickly to signal to them that a blue card = good, and a red card = bad.

Our unconscious minds work at high speed – before our conscious minds have even caught up – transforming signifiers into the basis upon which we make quick decisions designed to benefit us or, at least, keep us safe. When any of us comes into contact with a person, or an object, or a concept, the same thing happens: our unconscious minds, seeking to enable us to make quick and successful decisions about how we should relate to or feel about that person or object or idea, uses short cuts based on pre-existing knowledge we have stored in our brains. It means that all of us, depending on the nature of the stored knowledge we have, will make snap decisions we are not even aware we are making about how we should feel towards or relate to that person, object or concept, in order to do well out of the exchange and to stay 'safe'.

The important thing to say about unconscious bias at this point is that it is entirely normal and natural. All of us have unconscious bias and, based on our experiences and what we have been exposed to throughout our lives, all of us will have a uniquely positioned set of characteristics we are biased towards and others we are biased against. So it may be you share some biases with me, perhaps because we are of a similar age, grew up in the same culture or country, come from a similar class background, are of the same gender, or had common educational experiences. But, of course, there will also be other biases you don't share with me, or that you possess and I don't. That's because no two people have lived identical lives, and even if the key features are the same, the detail will be different. So I may find myself drawn to someone upon meeting them because, unconsciously, they remind me of a kindly neighbour I knew as a child. You didn't know that neighbour so may not feel as immediately trusting of or warm towards that person as I do.

Depiction versus reality

To take this a step further: we're constantly surrounded not just by real people, but by *depictions* of other people – on TV, film, in the pages of our newspapers, in books and magazines, on billboards, and on the screens of our devices. Just as our unconscious brains store information about the people we meet in reality – my kindly neighbour, for instance – they also store information about the people we encounter through these depictions.

Regardless of whether these people are real or fictional, whether I'm looking at a screen and seeing Bill Clinton or *The West Wing's* Jed Bartlet, I will on an unconscious level take some information about US Presidents from the way these two men are depicted. If we say that the nature of our unconscious bias is in part informed by what we are exposed to by, say, the depictions of groups of people as well as the people we *actually* come into contact with throughout our lives, then it's fair to say that the way different types of people are depicted – or even *not* depicted – is incredibly important and goes some way towards explaining why some groups, in the theatre industry, and beyond, do better than others.

To look at this purely in gender terms, there are many studies that demonstrate that, when it comes to depictions of different people in the media, there are marked differences between the manner and frequency with which men and women feature. Add in other factors like the age or the ethnicity of women and the differences become even more pronounced. The Geena Davis Institute on Gender in Media conducts massive studies analysing groups of newly released Hollywood movies. They've found really bizarre things: like that the ratio of male to female characters in family movies is 3:1 and that, even more strangely, women make up only 17 per cent of characters in crowd scenes; that of characters with jobs, 81 per cent are male; that only 10 per cent of films across the ten most profitable film markets have gender-balanced casts, i.e. where women make up 45 to 55 per cent of characters.

There is evidence to suggest that being exposed to female characters being typically depicted in one way and male characters in another is something we get used to at a very young age. A University of California study from the early 2000s looked at depictions of male and female characters in children's TV cartoons. They found that 'Behaviours that were relatively more likely among female characters across genres included showing fear, acting romantic, being polite, and acting supportive.' What all this means – if we follow the logic of unconscious bias – is that, having been exposed to these stories, we make all sorts of assumptions about whether a person is likely to show fear, act romantically, be polite, or act supportively, based on their gender.

Apparently we also apply such assumptions to a human from the earliest point in their life: a study was done where a video of a baby was watched by groups of volunteers. Some of the groups were told the baby was male, others that the baby was female, and others that the baby was intersex. Overwhelmingly, when asked to describe the baby's behaviour, those who had been told it was male used attributes and qualities traditionally associated with masculine behaviour to describe it, while those told it was female overwhelmingly used descriptors that are traditionally identified as feminine. Those who were told the baby was intersex tended to attribute both masculine and feminine descriptors to the baby in equal measure. Of course, all the groups watched the same video of the same infant, but being told what the baby's biological sex allegedly was had a significant impact on the impression they had of its character and behaviour.

The good and bad news about unconscious bias

Unconscious bias can work in our favour. If we're lucky, and the things people have been exposed to in relation to people like us are positive, we can actually benefit from their unconscious bias. It may provide us with a level of privilege we may not have otherwise had. We may be considered for opportunities or senior positions, not because we're necessarily better candidates than others, but because there is an assumption that we possess positive or desirable qualities, even if there is no evidence to back this up.

But conversely – and this is the nub of it – if the signifiers that others have received about people like us are negative, that can go against us. If, for instance, the biases they possess suggest people like us will be indecisive or weak, catty or divisive, stupid or inarticulate, lacking in judgement or emotional to the point of professional incompetence, then that set of assumptions – even if not in the conscious part of an interviewer's mind – may be enough to mean that we are passed over for a job in favour of a candidate who, walking through the door, brings with them a set of positive associations in the unconscious mind of the interviewer. Because these biases trigger in the interviewer a feeling that placing trust in this person will be a 'safe' decision.

It's also worth pointing out that unconscious bias can influence not just how we respond to others, but also how we feel about ourselves. If we are routinely exposed to signifiers that affirm and celebrate people like us, the short cuts our unconscious brain makes can say 'Hey, I'm bound to be pretty cool too.' But it can go the other way and this can kick in from a young age. To return to children's TV, a study was done in the US which plotted over several years the levels of self-esteem in children against the amount of television they watched. The children involved in the study were split into four groups: black boys, white boys, black girls, and white girls. The researchers found that as television viewing increased so self-esteem proportionally decreased in all but one group of children in the sample: the white boys. Theirs increased with the more television they watched.

Unconscious bias in action

I observed what could probably be described as unconscious bias in action about ten years ago; at the time I didn't know what it was and it was only years later, when I learned about unconscious bias, that I could put a name to what, I suspect, was going on. At the time I was in rehearsals in a theatre that, later in the year, was to produce a large-scale show featuring a choir made up of young people selected from across the local area. The music was classical and would be demanding, so the audition process for this choir was being taken seriously and the theatre was running individual as well as group auditions. It was the end of a day of rehearsals and I was finishing off some paperwork when the musical director arrived with a rehearsal pianist and let me know he would shortly be commencing some one-to-one choir auditions, but if I'd like to stay in the room working I'd be very welcome to do so. So I did.

Once the auditions got underway a series of young people individually entered the room, sang the same set piece, responded to a few notes from the MD, did a bit of chat with him and then left. Between each audition, the MD would speak his thoughts aloud to the pianist on each auditionee. He'd comment first on their technical ability (which I didn't have the musical knowledge myself to make head nor tail of), but then he'd move on to his reading of their personalities, the level of commitment he thought they'd bring, and their suitability for being a member of the choir on a quite pressurised yet prestigious production.

What I couldn't help but notice was that those young people who, by outward appearances, came from working-class backgrounds – for instance, whose school uniforms were sweatshirts and polo shirts, who spoke with a certain accent and used a particular vocabulary, and wore their hair and make-up in certain ways – were more likely to be assessed by the MD as having personalities that made them unsuitable for the choir: 'She looked like a troublemaker', 'I'm not sure how committed that one would be' and 'I just don't know if her attitude is right' are the sort of comments he would make. He seemed like a nice enough guy and he clearly knew his stuff on the musical front. But in terms of his response to the young people as individual human beings – and whether he felt they belonged in his choir – there was clearly something at play.

Of course, that thing may have been plain and straightforward snobbishness and if I'd have raised it with him he might have said that yes, he was consciously assembling an exclusively middle-class choir. Or it may have been something deeper, something less conscious. I doubt many of these particular young people he had concerns about were given places in the choir. That wasn't neccessarily because they were weaker singers, but perhaps simply because their school uniforms, or jewellery, or hairstyles, or accents, fired in the unconscious mind of the MD images and memories of other young people he'd seen depicted, perhaps on TV or in the news, that also had these things. If, in these depictions, those young people were generally shown to be lazy, argumentative, disrespectful, disruptive – 'troublemakers' – that may have skewed the perception he had of such young people when encountering them in the audition scenario. I remember leaving that room feeling incredibly sad because a place in that choir was something that clearly had the potential to be a profoundly enriching experience for the young people who were given the opportunity. But I could see all too clearly which of those wouldn't be in with a chance.

The problem with unconscious bias is just that: it's unconscious

The MD, had he thought about it with his conscious mind, might well have been horrified to discover he was so biased against young people who appeared to be from a particular background. He may have considered himself to be a lovely, liberal, open-minded person, and who knows, with his conscious mind in gear he might well have striven to possess and exhibit these values in his thoughts and deeds. But it's worth remembering that unconscious bias is just that: unconscious.

When we encounter a person for the first time, unconscious bias is at work, despite what we feel is at the forefront of our conscious mind or the values that we may hold dear. There's something called an IAT (Implicit Association Test) which was developed to test unconscious bias. You can take some of these tests online. Just out of interest I took some myself recently about women in the workplace and the result was interesting. I'm a woman myself, I've chosen to work, and not just to work but to do so with the aim of promoting the benefits of gender equality, and I'm a committed feminist. In spite of all this, my score results were pretty shocking. Apparently I have quite clear unconscious bias against women holding jobs rather than being homemakers, and especially if those jobs are in the realms of science and technology. It seems the depictions of women I've been surrounded by my entire life have wormed their way into my unconscious, regardless of what my conscious brain tells me to believe about women's capacity to hold an equal place to men in the world of work.

Taking Steps to Address Unconscious Bias

So what do we do about this? Earlier I said that unconscious bias is normal and natural – and it is. We can't beat ourselves up about it or feel guilty for possessing it. Where, however, we can come in for criticism is if, once recognising that as human beings we are biased towards certain people and against others, we take no steps to check ourselves when making decisions that may impact on other people, or we fail to acknowledge that our receptors may not be as brilliantly attuned as we think they are.

The importance of challenging our unconscious bias

Many of us involved in theatre are responsible for selecting people to receive opportunities of some sort. Whether that's auditioning performers, selecting team members to work alongside us, employing new members of staff, or choosing individuals to receive awards or have their work showcased publicly. In fact, the constantly shifting nature of who is working where and in what capacity in theatre means that it's an industry in which a higher than average number of people are involved in processes around selecting beneficiaries of opportunity and resource. To take the idea further, on even the most basic level, each of us decides what work we will go to see; whether, for instance, we dedicate our money and our time to supporting the work of playwright X by buying a ticket to their show, or playwright Y.

What this means is that we all have a particular duty, and vested interest, in remaining aware of the fact that we have unconscious bias and to check ourselves so that we are making decisions based on merit and considered thought, not the short cuts our brain instinctively takes. That might be as simple as asking ourselves straightforward questions when reaching a fork in a road. For instance, why are there certain shows we're automatically disinterested in when looking in a theatre's brochure and others we're quickly drawn towards? Is there something about the subject matter or the characteristics of the artists involved that emanates from our unconscious rather than conscious brain and, if so, should we perhaps make the choice to expose ourselves to the work we were originally less drawn to, thereby broadening our experience and tastes? Or, if we feel one person is a 'safe' choice and another a 'risky' choice in an employment or casting scenario, what is that based on? Can it be articulated in words or is it a 'gut' feeling? If it's the latter, would it be worth reflecting on a bit longer?

Why theatre is particularly susceptible to unconscious bias

Of course, unconscious bias is a feature of every workplace and cuts across every industry. But there are certain features of how theatre works that makes it an environment in which unconscious bias has the potential to play a particularly big role in affecting who does and doesn't receive opportunities. Beyond the speed with which we're generally trying to get everything done, there's the informal nature of the networks around which theatre operates and, by extension, the somewhat irregular approach to recruitment and commissioning that can occur. We generally have a quick turnover of staff and workers, because so much of what we do is short-term or project/production-based. A significant proportion of theatre workers are on freelance or short-term engagements, meaning that recruitment and sourcing of talent needs to happen quickly because it is so frequent.

In this context, making 'safe' choices can feel particularly important. When you know what you're going to get, and when you're having to assemble a team quickly, hit the ground running from the first day of rehearsals, and trust that you will all be speaking the same language throughout a process, it's highly appealing to assemble a group of people like you, or on your 'wavelength'. When you're 'only as good as your last show', or the fixed-term contract you're on is one you hope will be renewed, or there's no capacity in your team for mopping up should anything go wrong, the fear of the unknown – including people who aren't like you, or who might tackle tasks differently to you, or who express themselves in a way that feels mysterious to you – can feel too risky to countenance.

The outcome of this is that whenever new people are being sought out – whether that's a new Chair of the Board, additions to the pool of casual technical staff, or members of the onstage youth choir – it's incredibly easy for them to resemble the people who are already to be found in that environment. Their very familiarity is what has made them so appealing to the people who have recruited them. Likewise, people are positioned in places not necessarily as a result of where their individual skills, talents and interests actually lie, but because that's where the depictions of people like them suggest they should be. So – to use a blunt example – women are channelled into and encouraged towards supportive, nurturing, 'soft' skill-based roles; men into leadership, technical or 'uncompromising yet inspired artistic genius' roles.

Slowing down

A lot of the work we all need to do to counter this is about slowing down our decision-making processes. Or at least building in more time, or including more people in the process of reaching a decision before a choice is made. That won't be easy; time is a rare, valuable and often elusive commodity in theatre. If we can work out how to deal with the time issue (and while not necessarily without challenge, this certainly isn't impossible), being alert to, and acting with an awareness of our inevitable unconscious bias can be one of the greatest tools we can use to address the imbalances in theatre. There must be some more imaginative ways for us to get to know one another than we're currently using, it's just down to us now to imagine them. What, for instance, is the preferable alternative to the fifteen-minute audition slot, during which a director hardly has time to see an actor act, let alone understand what makes them tick as an artist or a human being? How can we rethink those all-important coffee meetings so we can assess what each party would bring to a working relationship rather than only what we unconsciously assume they will, or how much we instinctively like one another? What's the process for deciding whether a piece of work gets commissioned, or wins an award, or goes on the main stage rather than in the studio – and can that process include a plethora of opinions and perspectives rather than those of just one or two people?

While theatre is a working environment that is often moving at great speed, and in which there's a high frequency of decisions being made at any one time, the insertion of a moment to stop and think about why we're instinctively making the choices we are is a crucial one. Consistently inserting a moment to think with our conscious brain could be what is required to break away from our unconscious bias and make new decisions in different directions.

Art

It will come as no surprise to you, although I think it's worth reminding ourselves because sometimes those things hidden in plain sight are the hardest to spot, that the majority of the art we've inherited has been created by men, about men. Notice the use of the word *inherited* here. I'm not saying that the majority of the art made up to this point in human history was created by men, nor about them. I'm saying the majority of it is that's in our consciousness, which we know of and have been taught to consider important.

The lady's art vanishes

How many works by dead women will you see displayed on the walls of the National Gallery? Performed at the Royal Opera House? Sold on the shelves of the classic fiction section of Waterstones? Not many – yes, a few – but nowhere near the number of those by dead men (and dead white men at that). I've failed as yet to find any conclusive scientific evidence that men are biologically better engineered to create art, and I don't believe en masse they are more artistically inclined than women. So why so few female artists in our awareness? How many did *you* study at school?

Of course, it doesn't take much to explain the reasons behind the dearth of female artists in our collective consciousness: for whole swathes of history, women were barely considered capable of rational thought, so it's little wonder they weren't taken seriously as artists. Implicit in this is the lack of economic value that was generally attached to most artistic works by women. From the moment humans began daubing paint on their cave walls we can safely assume that as many women as men (of a certain class at least, as soon as class became a factor in the human experience) had the impulse to be creative – that they painted, or composed music, or wrote poetry. But women's artistic pursuits would largely have been considered hobbies rather than careers or vocations. Because of this, their work was rarely commodified, largely remained restricted to the domestic sphere and consequently often went unrecorded.

This lack of economic value attached to art by women accounts in no small part for its comparative invisibility today. If a painting has been purchased from a professional artist it is more likely to be cared for by its owner and, the higher the price paid for the painting, the greater the likelihood of it being passed down to future generations who, in turn, look after it carefully. A painting, perhaps of an equal level of artistic quality, but produced as someone's 'hobby', would be less likely guaranteed to survive in this way. At best, old Aunt Elspeth's watercolours might be held on to for sentimental value by the generation or two after her but beyond that, who knows? On the rare occasions that art created by women was deemed of commercial interest, the survival rates are much greater, but still only show us a tiny part of what must have been a far fuller picture: Jane Austen and the Brontë sisters would not have been the only women writing high-quality literature in the 1800s.

The low social value accorded to women impacted on a low monetary value being attached to their work, hindering the chances that these pieces of art would survive to the present day. Add to this a general dismissal of women's experiences and ideas as having any kind of importance or value – a dismissal which, for centuries, was the largely unchallenged norm – and it's not difficult to see why the records of their artistic output are significantly more limited than those of men.

Different types of 'great' and the benefits of diversity among artists

The fact that women's work has, in the main part, not made it into today's canon of 'great art' is something that poses a challenge to any art form, including theatre, that wants to become more equitable in terms of gender. Instinctively we understand ourselves through what has gone before; we look to our heritage, and the 'greats' of our past to be able to articulate where we have reached today. When we search for markers of 'quality' against which to measure new artistic works, the places we tend to look to – often the most prestigious or visible spaces, such as the walls of the National Gallery, the stages of the Royal Opera House, or the classics section of a branch of Waterstones – are almost exclusively populated by work that is male and white. Yes, it may be brilliant. But it only reflects one quite narrow type of brilliance. And when just one type of brilliance is put on display it's very easy to assume there is only one kind of brilliance that exists, or at least that matters.

To issue a disclaimer: what I'm not saying here is that men are biologically hard-wired to paint, or compose, or write, or design in one way and women in another. Rather, I am making the point that any piece of art in some way reflects the circumstances of the person who creates it, whether that be their cultural heritage, age, class, personal experiences, politics, beliefs, identity, gender, sexuality, or an infinite variety of other factors that make them who they are. What makes the possibilities of art so thrilling is that no two pieces can ever be identical because no two artists are. If you were to commission a poet in their eighties to compose a collection with the title *Memories*, they would almost certainly come up with a very different response to a poet in their twenties. Similarly, if you were to look at the work of a poet who has lived life in a female body – and has experienced everything, good and bad, that may come with that – you would likely find elements, or possibly even a whole personality to the work, that you wouldn't had it been written by someone who has experienced the world as a man.

A while back I was visiting Chatsworth House in Derbyshire, the stately home owned by the Duke and Duchess of Devonshire. I was there with a friend who was working at Chatsworth as a tour guide at the time and, despite that being his day off, he'd offered to take me round the house and gave me my own informal guided tour. The Devonshire family, who have lived at Chatsworth since the 1550s, have for many generations been avid commissioners and collectors of art, and the house is crammed with a stunning range of paintings, drawings and sculptures, including the current inhabitants' collection of contemporary art on the ground floor. On the remaining floors, the walls heave under the older works. As my friend and I walked around this part of the collection, we turned a corner and I was confronted with the most unexpected painting I'd clapped eyes on all afternoon. It looked from its execution like something from the 1700s, and yet in its form was more like a hybrid of a *Flower Fairies* illustration, a still from a Kate Bush video, and the album cover of a 1970s prog-rock band. It showed a woman (I later found out, Georgiana the Duchess of Devonshire depicted as Cynthia in Spenser's *The Faerie Queen*, and painted in 1781–82) suspended in the air amid a halo of cloud and moonlight, seemingly flying straight towards the viewer, hand outstretched. It was so different to the other countless portraits of aristocracy

I'd seen that day: no better, no worse, just *different*. 'Do you know,' my friend told me, 'it's the only painting outside of the contemporary collection that's by a woman.'

To me this moment encapsulates the benefits of diversity among artists; if you have a variety of artists coming at things from a range of perspectives, experiences and walks of life, they will inevitably interpret the same subject in a different way and that, in turn, gives us a wider range of artistic products to enjoy. Maria Hadfield Cosway, the artist of the painting that had so caught my eye, *Georgiana as Cynthia*, had interpreted both her subject, a member of the English aristocracy, and the format in which she was working, portraiture, in a fundamentally different way to every other artist on display in the upper halls and corridors of the house. Can we say that's because she lacked a Y chromosome? Probably not. But did her experience of the world, living in a woman's body, with all the social and cultural expectations attached to that, have an impact on how she chose to depict the Duchess? Very likely. Might she, as a fellow woman, have been able to develop a relationship with her subject not possible had she been a man and did this inform the context in which she positioned Georgiana on the canvas? Quite possibly. It certainly looked like it.

Among the historical collection at Chatsworth, Hadfield Cosway's work jumped out as both refreshing and unexpected. It prompted me to think differently about a particular member of the aristocracy – depicted as she was flying through the air – to how I had thought of all the others I had gazed upon, sat stiffly in their family groupings, or on horseback surveying their lands. It also made me re-evaluate what I thought I knew about late-eighteenth-century European portraiture because this was unlike anything I had seen from that period before. I had a similarly invigorating experience a year or so back, in a different art form, when I saw Matthew Bourne's all-male version of *Swan*

Lake (yes, I know I was about twenty years late to the party) and was struck to see the duet between Odette and the Prince danced not, as I had always previously seen it, by a man and a woman, but by two men: seeing two bodies practically identical in physical size and strength doing lifts that were different to those traditionally performed by male/female pairs. Again, I'm not making a value judgement that these dancers' performances, or the choreography of the *pas de deux* were any better or worse than versions of the dance I had seen previously, but making the point that they were *different*. That opened up new perspectives for me in regards to how I viewed the relationship between those two characters in that well-known narrative, and also what classical ballet can be and what it can look like.

Having a range of artists, and therefore art, on offer to us has always felt like a good thing to me, because when I go to the theatre, or an art gallery, or a cinema, I want to be confronted by a range of stories, perspectives, voices and ideas. Sometimes it feels important and reassuring to me to encounter art made by someone whose experience of the world correlates with my own. But I don't only want to see my own values and experiences reflected back at me; I want to witness art that offers me windows into other worlds, other lives, other ages, other societies, other civilisations, other opinions. I don't just want to see the same kind of artistic product, or the same stories told, by the same sort of person, over and over again.

Attributing excellence

So, in this light, how do we broaden the range of art, and artists, which we take seriously? One of the key things for us to put under the microscope if we are to move forward in this respect are the mechanisms by which we attribute artistic value.

How do we decide what art and which artists are 'excellent'? What is that based on? Deciding what does and doesn't get included in a definition of 'great' art isn't an empirical exercise. It's not like compiling a sporting hall of fame, itself tricky, but at least one can look back over history for the races run fastest, the javelins thrown farthest, or the points scored quickest. Attributing exceptional status to art is a far more mercurial thing, largely because everyone's tastes are their own and what seems exceptional in one person's eyes is mediocre in another's. There are no hard-and-fast rules for defining what does and doesn't denote quality in a piece of art, only a shifting set of values – often informed by fashions and contemporary social mores – against which we make our decisions.

I used to do a fair amount of script-reading for various theatres to earn extra cash around my directing. Generally this would involve being sent a batch of plays that had been submitted to the theatres, often unsolicited, but perhaps by members of an in-house writers' group or in response to a playwriting competition. Usually I'd be asked to write a short report on each script and send it back to the theatre with some kind of recommendation, variously 'No thank you', 'Not right for us but please send us your next play', or 'This is good, recommend for further attention'. Today, when I look back to how I dealt with the activity of reading plays, I do think there was something less than perfect in the templates I was using to outline what my recommendation for each would be.

I think – I fear – that when I sat down to make my way through my latest batch of scripts, I would be quite quick to make a judgement about which of the three catagories a play fell into. What was that decision based on? I have a suspicion that it was a pre-existing checklist that was in my head of 'what makes a good play'. It was a checklist I had learned, one that had been taught to me by a variety of sources: through the plays I was given to study at school and during my drama degree (and therefore assumed were important, *because* they had been given to me to study); through looking at what sorts of writing got put on in big or high-profile theatres; through listening to the language my older and more experienced colleagues used to dissect plays in the bar after a show; through the theatre reviews I diligently read in the newspapers.

At the time it never occurred to me to stop and question where my tastes were coming from or how they might be skewed towards certain types of work and away from others. While I remain pretty confident that the majority of plays I dismissed as 'no thank you's deserved that, there are others I wonder about; those I didn't have a quick and easy reference point for and so dropped on to the rejection pile. Were there some scripts among the hundreds I read that I speedily dismissed not because they were bad, but because they were different to what I was conditioned to consider 'good'? Maybe it wasn't that they weren't good, it's just that they were a *different type* of good to what I had been trained to look out for.

Being open to a wider range of 'good'

If we're genuine about our desire to see greater equality in theatre, we'll need to be open to a wider range of 'good': more varied style, genre, form and content appearing on our stages. If we broaden the pool of artists beyond the one quite homogenous group that has to date dominated it, that will inevitably broaden the type of work we get to see. This is, of course, a good thing and very exciting for theatre.

But – and it's a big but – whether, once we have opened our stages up to difference, this work will 'survive' to be inherited by the next generation, or even receive the scale of platform it deserves today, depends largely on us recalibrating the ways we attribute levels of value and artistic quality to art and artists. Because if we judge all work by the metrics we've traditionally used to identify what is and isn't 'great' – metrics which only respond to a narrow range of art and artists – it's unlikely we'll ever make it past the first post of our initial enthusiasm for greater equality and diversity. 'Ah,' we'll say, 'we did *try* to shift the balance towards non-white men. The problem was so few of them were any *good*.'

Until we think long and hard about the nature of our artistic heritage and how it informs our contemporary artistic identity, we can't look to the future with any certainty that our industry's artistic outputs will be any more diverse than they currently are. This is because we are likely to keep replicating what we have previously, in our limited experience, been brought up to think is the definition of 'good'. Central to this, we must be honest about the extent to which our heritage was constructed as a result of a system predicated on significantly over-favouring artists from one relatively small demographic while essentially failing to recognise artists from any other, and only then on limited terms.

How do we begin this process? One of the first things we can do is begin to be a little more circumspect about the art we've inherited. We can continue to enjoy, respect and be moved by its brilliant elements, its beauty and its craft. We should continue staging and displaying it. But we should also recognise that it is not the complete story of what great art is.

We should also scrutinise what the canonical works of art say to us. We need to notice where they fall short or where the messages carried by this work no longer reflect what we want to say about and to the world. Yes, these works of art were often created before a time when women were expected to be equal players in society, and so are simply windows on to a different era. But they're still there, on public display, still influencing how we think and feel about ourselves, and the opposite gender. And that, if we're not aware of it, impacts on where we derive our artistic tastes from today and what stories we continue to tell. We should also think more fully about what our relentless trumpeting of these works above all others does to women trying to work in the arts. I speak with the experience of someone who's directed a lot of classics when I say it's hard if the work you're engaging in depicts people like you as bit-part players, stupid or weak. Those messages have a tendency of sometimes coming out in behaviour of others towards you, inside and outside the rehearsal room.

This process may feel from the outset like one of loss, of jettisoning much-loved works of art, but it's really not. I'm not suggesting we banish *The Pickwick Papers*, or *The Wind in the Willows*, or *Jesus Christ Superstar* from our cultural landscape. What I'm saying is that we now need to *add* to those works and have an open mind towards pieces that aren't like them. Just because a piece of work doesn't resemble what we have been taught to believe is 'great', doesn't mean that it's not. There are many different types of 'great'. It's just that previously the world wasn't organised in such a way that recognised some of these.

This won't necessarily be easy. As I stood in the corridor at Chatsworth House looking up at *Georgiana as Cynthia*, a couple wandered up behind me and paused briefly to look up at the painting. 'I don't know what *that* is,' one of them said in a dismissive tone, and they ambled on their way. When we don't understand something because we don't have a reference point for it, it's very easy to say it isn't any good. For theatres that need to balance the books, presenting their own theatrical equivalents of *Georgiana as Cynthia* can feel scary, and the prospect of an auditorium of variously blank-faced, disgruntled, or downright angry critics and audience members – or, even worse, an empty auditorium – is too risky for some to bear. It is a brave but vital act in which some theatres will feel better equipped and determined to lead the way than others. But over the last few years I've seen some – like the Royal Court, the Royal Exchange, and the Tricycle – be at the vanguard of this championing of new stories and new ways of telling stories by and about women, and have been so deeply inspired by what they are doing. I hope that the richness and dynamism of their artistic programmes, not to mention the considerable box-office success much of their work has enjoyed, will embolden others to follow suit.

Expanding our tastes – and our minds

If we can become broader-minded about what excellent theatre can be, the possibilities are endless and exciting: we will have expanded the repertoire immeasurably; ensured a greater diversity of work for our audiences to experience; made space for a wider range of stories and perspectives to challenge and inspire us; opened up to new ideas and ways of thinking about the world coming into our rehearsal rooms and offices, as well as on to our stages. It could lead to us entirely rethinking the models around how we make theatre, and what that theatre looks like and says both to and about the world. It could be the springboard for one of the most exciting artistic revolutions theatre has ever known.

At the very least, it would be a wonderful learning opportunity. To speak from personal experience, I know that going through the process of conducting the research for my first book, *100 Great Plays for Women*, broadened my own theatrical horizons significantly, along with my conception of what dramatic writing can be and do. The activity, which the research forced me to do, of reading plays that fell outside my pre-existing sphere of knowledge, or that I may have considered outside of my tastes, or which I probably wouldn't otherwise have read because for whatever reason I didn't consider them relevant to me, was a huge learning curve. Despite having previously considered myself very well read – and indeed, for years I'd been tearing through plays almost compulsively – I discovered there was a far broader range of material out there than I'd known about – because while I'd been reading lots of plays, they often tended to be the *same kinds* of plays. My goal with *100 Great Plays for Women* was to assemble a purposefully eclectic range of works for many different tastes, and as part of that I had to be able to articulate what made each of them worthy of the title 'great'. To do this I had to take time to understand why others may love them, even if I, on initial reading, didn't. As it was, taking the time to do so meant I ended up falling in love with those plays myself.

I'll finish this section with a conversation I had with a playwright a few years ago. I was interviewing him as part of a research study Tonic was doing at the time into opportunities for girls taking part in youth drama, with a particular focus on the type of roles available to them. The writer was musing over the differences between writing male and female characters in view of how we currently think of drama. He told me about having been commissioned a few years earlier to write two parallel monologues for young audiences, one to be performed by the character of a teenage boy, the other by the character of a teenage girl. The boy's monologue, he said, he found far more straightforward to write. It's a generalisation he observed, but often when teenage boys are under pressure (and what, after all, is drama if not someone under pressure of some sort or another?) they demonstrably *do* stuff: they kick, shout, punch, mouth off. This external display of emotion he described as being 'the meat and veg of dramatic writing'. When it came to writing the girl's monologue, he said he found it far more challenging. Again, a generalisation, he pointed out, but broadly speaking, when a teenage girl is under pressure she will internalise, meaning outward signs of her distress will be consciously limited or carefully concealed. All the 'action' going on is happening on the inside. What then, he found himself asking, is conventionally dramatic about that? The girl's piece, he said, although initially far harder to conceive, emerged as the significantly more interesting for him to write: he had to work out how to explode thirty seconds of one character's internal thought process into a half-hour piece of live performance. This, he said, was unlike anything he had written before.

I left this conversation buzzing. My goodness, I thought, there is so much dramatic terrain we've not even begun to explore yet as an art form; so many ways of constructing and telling stories that we've only just scratched the surface of; so many possible routes for dramatic form and structure and style to take – if only we open ourselves up to expand on who's doing the telling or through whose eyes the story is seen.

Artistic versus Admin Roles

Something that can make combating gender inequalities in theatre difficult is, perversely, the fact that there are so many women involved in theatre. Theatre has no lack of women keen to engage whether professionally, as amateur participants, students of the subject, or as audience members. The sheer volume of women can mask the fact that, while the numbers of women involved are incredibly healthy, profound imbalances exist in terms of where they are most likely to be concentrated within the industry, in what particular jobs, and at what level of resourcing and seniority.

It's a picture that is a complex one. The reasons behind the comparative lack of women in one area compared to another are nuanced and specific. Often there will be root causes in common, but generally there will be a wide range of differing factors that are distinct, informed by things such as the working culture within a certain area of the industry, the nature of a particular role, or the entry and progression routes in a specific field. Picking each of these apart would be a book in itself. So for now I'm going to take a broad look at just one key area of imbalance that currently exists, and a particularly important one: the division of men and women into artistic and administrative roles in professional theatre, and particularly at the top level.

Where have all the women gone?

I've been involved in theatre since I was tiny. Drama classes, youth theatre, school plays, Drama at GCSE, BTEC, and degree level: you name it, I was doing it. As a young adult I crewed at my local theatre, shifting the scenery and operating the follow-spot for amateur theatre companies, and began teaching drama to children myself. In every one of these scenarios there was one thing that was consistent: the number of female participants always significantly outstripped the number of male.

So I was surprised, upon eventually reaching professional rehearsal rooms, to find the opposite was true: repeatedly the number of men taking part exceeded the number of women. Yes, the stage-management team often tended to be female, and set and costume designers seemed to be women roughly half the time. But in terms of everyone else in the room – the actors and the rest of the creative-team members – it was like the ratio of men to women had been flipped. Where had all the girls and women gone who I'd watched rehearse scenes and paint scenery and put musical numbers up on their feet in the school halls and community centres of my childhood and adolescence? Why were women now the minority?

A short walk out of the rehearsal room and into the admin offices of a theatre and I found where the women had ended up: largely behind desks. I'm not dismissing a desk job in theatre (I myself traded in a rehearsal-room-based job for an office-centred one when I put aside directing to run Tonic), but still it was puzzling. I'd never noticed a lack of interest in artistic roles among my fellow females when we were taking part in theatre on an *amateur* level. Why, apparently were they suddenly so keen to leave that to the guys and get behind a desk when it came to being involved in *professional* theatre?

What I'm *not* saying here is that women don't work in artistic roles in theatre. They do. The industry is full of women who write, act, direct, design, choreograph and compose. I am also *not* saying that they don't make work. They do. However, the point is that when it comes to who is making work on the biggest, best resourced, and/or most visible professional stages in our country, women are significantly less likely than men to be getting those jobs.

As an indicator: in September 2014, Tonic hosted a big industry event on gender equality in theatre. We decided to do a bit of number-crunching in advance of the event to gain a snapshot of the situation for women. We counted up the number of men and women in artistic roles in all plays on stage in London's West End, and in the twenty theatres across England that were in receipt of the highest proportion of Arts Council funding on the Saturday night prior to the event. The numbers were pretty dismal. In the West End, women accounted for just 29 per cent of directors, 29 per cent of performers, 30 per cent of designers, 20 per cent of lighting designers (although this was one person lighting four different productions) and zero sound designers. Agatha Christie's *The Mousetrap* was the sole play by a woman on stage in the West End that night. The theatres in receipt of the highest proportion of public funds didn't fare much better. Of those that had a professional show on that night, women formed 38 per cent of directors, 8 per cent of writers, 37 per cent of performers, 22 per cent of lighting designers, and 17 per cent of sound designers. The only field in which women outnumbered men was in design in the subsidised theatres, with women representing 57 per cent of the total.

The balance of women and men across administrative and artistic roles – and why it matters

Sometimes when I'm speaking with the leaders of theatres about the potential for them to work with Tonic, I'll be politely turned down with an explanation along the lines of 'we're already a very female organisation'. A quick look on the staff list on their website will certainly confirm that yes, in terms of who's working in administrative areas – by which I include fields such as general management, finance, producing, fundraising and marketing – it certainly is. Do a scan of who's being employed by them in artistic roles though – to perform, direct, design or write the productions that their audiences get to see – and often it's the inverse. Sometimes I've worked with theatres that have been quite shocked when they've done a simple tally of how many men compared to women they've employed in artistic roles over the past few years, finding it to be significantly less balanced than they'd thought it would be. It's really easy, when from Monday to Friday the offices of your organisation are filled with women, not to clock that this doesn't automatically translate to the balance of the artistic programme your audience experiences in the evenings.

Some people will ask whether the gender imbalance between administrative and artistic roles matters. So long as there are roughly equal numbers of men and women in the theatre workforce as a total, is there a problem? I would argue though that it *is* worth our attention. When it comes to the direct interface between a theatre and the public – i.e. what an audience hears and sees when it sits in the auditorium – if the voices, ideas, stories and creativity of women aren't at the forefront of this in the same way as men's, then something isn't working as well as it could be. Beyond this, the currently imbalanced numbers would suggest that as an industry we're failing to spot or nurture some of our best theatre artists. All that passion for acting, directing, writing, designing, choreographing and composing exhibited by girls and young women at student and entry level can't be without merit. Somewhere along the way we must be letting artists with the potential to be excellent slip through our fingers.

But perhaps more than any other reason why it's important to note and address this particular imbalance is this: the greater likelihood of men taking up artistic roles and women administrative ones is something that filters upwards through organisations and finds expression at their top level; in leadership. That's of especial interest because, when it comes to establishing greater equality and diversity in any field, one of the best places to focus is on leadership. It is where power lies.

The impact at leadership level

In 2014, Tonic did some research into who was leading theatre organisations in the Arts Council's National Portfolio (the group of arts organisations that are in receipt of core funding from Arts Council England for the period April 2015 to March 2018). In terms of executive director (or equivalent) roles – i.e. the person who, broadly speaking, heads an organisation's administrative or operational side – women outnumbered men at 68 per cent to 32 per cent. The picture was different, though, in terms of artistic directors (or equivalent). When it came to who held the primary responsibility for deciding the artistic output of an organisation, just 37 per cent of these were women, with the number dropping to 24 per cent in organisations that received over £500,000 Arts Council England subsidy that year.

This is important because, when it comes to selecting an artistic programme and setting a creative agenda for an organisation, artistic directors hold the lion's share of decision-making powers. Executive directors, while having significant amounts of power and responsibility, essentially deliver that vision. What this means is that a large proportion of what makes its way on to public stages across the country is something that is heavily decided by the tastes, interests and passions of artistic directors. If people in artistic-director roles belong overwhelmingly to a single demographic – whatever that demographic may be – the artistic programmes that audiences have access to is less likely to be as broad and varied as it would be had it been created and curated by a less homogenous group of people.

Getting more women, and the broadest range of women, into artistic-director roles may feel like something few of us have control over. Ultimately, it's up to a theatre's board to decide who to appoint whenever its artistic-director post becomes available. Yet I would argue that there are a whole range of things that many of us can do to create shifts so that, cumulatively, we maximise promising individuals' potential to move into artistic-director roles, regardless of their gender. It goes without saying that we'll be building on a really strong foundation. The last five or so years has seen a significant new generation of female artistic directors coming into post – including at several key venues nationally – joining the ranks of trailblazers that have gone before them. The precedent is there; now we just need to work out how to expand on and consolidate it.

Learning from the Successes of Women in Administrative Leadership

As a powerful piece of ammunition, we can look to the positive example of women's success in attaining the most senior administrative leadership roles in theatre. The high proportion of women in executive-director-style leadership is one of the major good news stories of gender balance in theatre (one that isn't always acknowledged or celebrated as fully as it should be). So, given that we have an area that is seemingly very good at progressing women, let's look at what's working well there and consider how elements of that could be translated to how appointments and progression works for artistic directors. Because, while artistic and administrative leadership roles will always necessarily function in different ways and fulfil different needs, there must be learning we can draw from.

The first step in this will be to identify what the key differences are between how careers play out on the artistic side of theatre compared to the administrative side, and then beyond this, look at what it is about these two type of career structures that may either hinder or support women to progress. Of course, no two women, and no two women's careers, are identical, and it is impossible to say 'all women will struggle with this' or 'all women will be liberated by that'. But we can pay attention to generalised patterns and trends and, through this, begin to plot a way forward before then digging into the detail.

Freelancing versus salaried employment

One obvious headline, if we're looking for reasons why executive-director-style roles seem more straightforward for women to progress into than artistic-director roles, is that they are jobs that people generally graduate into from working in areas that usually entail being on salary and in permanent employment. Meanwhile, artistic-director roles almost unanimously go to people who have been artists (and generally directors), and so will have spent the overwhelming majority of their careers as freelancers. So someone who is in administrative leadership will most likely have benefitted throughout their working life from the protection and security of permanent contracts, sick pay, maternity leave, holiday pay, the ability to plan and budget over the long term, and a steady (and probably steadily increasing) income. That's something that most people in freelance artistic roles don't have. To be a freelancer is to be in a perpetual state of never knowing, of needing to drop things at a moment's notice if a job comes up, of having no guarantee of future work, of lacking a financial safety net, of having little flexibility or allowance made for taking time off for illness, pregnancy, caring commitments, or participating in activities outside your artistic practice.

I've been fascinated for some time now by the links between how freelancing works in theatre and the systemic underrepresentation of all sorts of people, including women in various parts of the industry. It's something that crystallised in my mind recently, while running the second iteration of Tonic's Advance programme. As part of the research phase of the programme, a colleague and I interviewed, ran focus groups with, and surveyed hundreds of people who are in freelance creative roles across theatre, dance and opera in the UK. Certain themes emerged again and again when people spoke about their careers. The challenges of freelancing was one that was particularly vivid. Here's how I wrote about it in Tonic's dissemination of the findings:

> Something the research underlined for us was how fragile careers in the performing arts are, and especially those of people in creative and/or freelance roles. To use an analogy:

if a career were a piece of rope suspended between two points, in many industries that rope would be relatively thick and strong. That's because it is made up of lots of individual strands that give it that strength – for instance, there may be a strand in place due to sick pay being there for someone to fall back on; another because there is the security of a permanent contract; another because the pay is consistently of a level that enables a person to cover their monthly outgoings. However, the piece of rope representing the career of a creative working in the performing arts may be significantly less sturdy. That's because many of the strands, such as those listed above, are unlikely to be in place (so it may instead resemble a frayed piece of rope, held together in just a few places). And if the rope becomes more depleted – through the loss of further strands – a great strain may be placed on those that remain, because proportionally there are fewer of them. It won't take the loss of too many more before a person may find their career is untenable; this is nothing to do with their talent or their commitment, just the circumstances in which they find themselves operating.

While this is the case for all but the most privileged creatives, the research suggested that women's careers are particularly likely to be characterised by severed strands. Earning on average less than male counterparts, being more likely to be programmed on smaller and lower-profile stages, more regularly encountering the biases that employers, critics and colleagues may consciously or unconsciously hold against them and their work, taking time off for caring responsibilities and pregnancy – these are just some of the factors that may compromise the integrity of a woman creative's career. Facing any number of these in combination (and it's worth remembering that some women will face far more than others) may be enough that a creative will feel her career isn't something she can, or wants to, continue with. At this point she may move into an associated field or role, one that provides her with a sturdier rope. She may remain lodged at a certain level of experience, feeling the base she's

operating on isn't robust enough from which to take the
leaps and risks often necessary to move to the next level. Or
she may simply walk away from the performing arts.

So to return to the subject of artistic directors, if women artists
stand a proportionally higher chance of operating with a 'frayed
rope', when it comes to the pool of candidates a board will be
recruiting from, there is an increased chance women won't be
there (because they've dropped out of the race before that point)
or their track records are less strong and not as full as those of
their male counterparts (because they've failed to progress to
the extent they may have done had the structure they were
working in been different). Again, to reiterate: all women are
different and those with a greater level of privilege or whose
personal circumstances happen to have played out in one
direction rather than another may find themselves with a
healthy number of strands in place. But there will be others –
perhaps not just because they are a parent but a *single* parent
(and when 91 per cent of single parents in the UK are women,
it's far more likely a female rather than male artist will be one),
or not just a woman but a woman of colour, or a woman from
a working-class background, or an older woman – who will be
negotiating multiple barriers before they can even get into a
rehearsal room, let alone to the top of the pile for a plum
artistic-director job.

There's also something that's deeply inhibiting on an artistic
level about operating with a frayed rope of a career. If, for
instance, a freelance director has cause to believe that their
career is already so fragile that one show poorly received by the
critics or a couple of months without work will tip it over the
edge into oblivion – or at least take it significantly closer to the
precipice – it's going to be far harder for them to be bold, to
take risks, to innovate; to do those things that, in short, we
often desire and demand in someone who becomes an artistic

director. It also makes it difficult for them to be picky about jobs, to hold out for those that are genuinely exciting or that will progress them artistically. Making pragmatic choices, like spending six months every year directing drama-school shows because it is properly paid and predictable, is not going to give a director the sort of public profile, reviews or awards that's going to make a board salivate over their CV.

Finally, if your rope is already frayed, dealing with the unconscious bias or prejudice other people hold against you and your work can take a particular toll. It's also something that as a freelancer you'll be coming up against on an unusually regular basis. For people who are salaried and hold permanent contracts, being met with bias or prejudice in a recruitment context is a very real but not necessarily frequent experience; once you've proven to an interview panel or your new team that you've got what it takes, that's something you've not got to go through again for at least a couple of years or whenever it is you choose to move on. But for a freelance director, there is the constant process of pitching for shows, winning over casts, enlisting creative teams and proving to technical crews you know your stuff – and this never ends. Freelancing is a bit like being the new kid at school, but moving to a new school every few weeks. This is something which, if you're different to most of the other kids in the school, or are not what they are expecting, can be particularly draining.

It's worth noting that some women (and men) will remove themselves from the usual progression routes to artistic-director positions by setting up their own companies, and leading them on their own terms. This is very liberating and empowering, but is not without significant challenges, least of all financial. There's a big difference between being the artistic director of your own company, one that maybe creates a couple of small-scale projects a year, and the artistic director of an established theatre organisation in receipt of several million pounds of public subsidy each year. Being the artistic director of a tiny non-core-funded theatre company can be just as precarious, and provide just as many challenges to women, as being a freelance artist.

My hunch is that, if the progression routes into administrative leadership did, like those into artistic leadership, rely on people having been successful freelancers, then women would be far less well-represented in executive-director roles too. That's not to say that the path to becoming an executive director isn't fraught with challenges, or that it is a level playing field. But because freelancing proportionally throws up greater challenges for women it is fair to say that it is also proportionally less likely they will be enabled, by the system as it currently works, to reach artistic-director roles.

Lack of structure

Another key area to which we should draw our attention when seeking to understand the differences between progression routes to administrative and artistic leadership, is how much less structured things are on the artistic side. Again, this is something that emerged as a strong theme in the Advance research Tonic conducted, both from what we heard from freelancers, and from what we learned about how many performing-arts organisations operate:

> The performing arts tend to favour an 'organic' way of working, especially in relation to the making of artistic works and the employment of creatives. Certain protocols, structures and procedures that are in place for employing and providing working conditions for people in most other industries (and even, to a certain extent, in the administrative side of the performing arts) aren't necessarily there. Instead,

there tends to be a less structured approach ('Whose work have we seen recently?' 'Who are people saying is "hot"?' 'Who's on our radar?'), based on a perception that when it comes to creatives, talent will inevitably make itself known.

The research findings suggest, however, that this lack of structure – however well-intentioned or benignly motivated it may be – is in part responsible for the pronounced imbalances that exist in terms of who is employed in creative roles, and at what scale. While the theory may be that operating free of conventional employment practices gives organisations/employers an unclouded vista from which they can identify the most exciting talent, in reality it is those people who are best adapted to thrive in this unstructured environment that will be the most visible; talent may be a secondary factor. So while employment practices used in other industries may not be directly applicable to the employment of creatives, devising and implementing structures which enable organisations to a) select creatives based on ability, not just visibility, and b) monitor whether they are genuinely catering to their needs once they are in the workplace, is an important part of the equation when addressing imbalances between men and women in creative areas.

There can be a misapprehension in theatre that if no structure is put in place, equality is created among artists; there is a clear, open field in which everyone has an equal chance to demonstrate their talent, make a play for resources, or stand a chance of progressing to senior roles (including artistic directorships). But in practice it doesn't work like that, because not everyone is starting from the same place. Some people have been more empowered than others, some will benefit from privilege that others don't, some will be more visible or have a greater voice than others do. So if we want to see a broader range of people progress into artistic-director roles, we do at times need to impose structure in regards to how we work with artists while they are on their way up, in order to create the level playing field that we don't naturally have.

We've recognised the value of doing this with staff on the administrative side of our organisations. We run proper recruitment processes and advertise jobs, rather than handing them out based on non-transparent decision-making to people within networks that have unclear entry points. We provide them with the opportunity to proactively seek out and participate in training and personal-development opportunities, rather than hazarding they'll accrue skills and knowledge along the way. We give them the freedom to take time off from their careers by ensuring the door is left propped open behind them through, for instance, structured maternity leave, rather than carelessly allowing it to bang shut. We do these things because we recognise that we'll get the most out of people, and the strongest workforces – including the strongest administrative leadership – if we are flexible to what people need in order to progress to the point where they are the best versions of themselves that they can be.

Structures that enable us to listen

We're also better at having structures in place so we can listen to and check in with administrative staff than we are with artists. While conducting the Advance research, I remember questioning one artistic director about the nature of communication channels that existed between him and the visiting freelance artists who made work in his organisation. Was there, for instance, anything similar to the exit interview that would be done when someone departs the administrative staff, with visiting artists after they finish a production? 'Oh no,' he said – in a tone I interpreted to mean that he felt it wouldn't be appropriate to ask artists to go through such a dry process – 'it's all very organic, they'll probably just come and have a chat in the bar afterwards if they want to.'

It is, I remember reflecting at the time, this tendency to leave things unquestioned and unsought for, and instead wait for them to come to you, that is part of the challenge facing those artists who are seeking to progress in a system that wasn't initially conceived with their needs in mind. Not everyone will feel empowered enough to strike up a conversation with an artistic director about what wasn't great about their experience working in his building. Indeed, some will have places they need to be in the evening, meaning they won't even be in the bar in the first place. But even if they are there and are happy to chat, isn't it crucial that the artistic director proactively invites feedback from the artist, rather than assuming that no news is good news? Because failing to elicit feedback from artists – or providing them with a structured manner in which to give it – implies the way you work is fine, and if the artist experienced difficulties with it, they are the ones who are deficient. It also means that barriers experienced by certain groups of artists are likely to be perpetuated, because nothing has been put in place either to recognise or address them.

Creating structures for artists

It's not workable to graft practices and structures designed for the permanent staff in an administrative team directly on to those on the artistic side. But there are elements that could be carried across, albeit in an adapted form. Take the exit interview example I outlined above. There must be productive ways that theatres could generate useful feedback from visiting artists, and do so in a way that isn't time-draining, or sterile, or puts anyone in an awkward or combative situation. It would be a creative, engaging and important part of the broader production process, one which benefits the artist, making them reflect on what they want to do to improve their practice going forward, as much as it does the theatre. It would be an unusual collaboration, but I'd be fascinated to see what a general manager or an HR director working with a group of artists on this for a couple of days emerged with. Quite possibly something that would be stimulating and nourishing for theatres and artists alike, not dull or perfunctory.

Returning to the issues around freelance careers, there is, I think, space for the industry to consider how freelance artists could – not all the time but some of the time – benefit from the opportunities that permanent employment offers. As an industry we're really mindful to offer one-year bursaries or six-month residencies to emerging artists, people entering the industry, or those under a certain age. These provide a range of benefits: financial stability (even if only for a few months), a regular place of work and the opportunity to 'belong' somewhere, access to networks and relationship-building, an insight into how an organisation functions, and so on. These are really positive interventions, but I think as an industry we have a tendency to view them like rocket fuel; that they give a young person's career an initial boost, but beyond that, if they are any good, they will continue to ascend from there under their own momentum.

Not all artists' lives – or careers – pan out like that, and some need 'boosts', or the chance to regroup or refuel, or have the space to increase their skills, or the freedom to take some risks, at later points. Some, for instance, would like to stop and start their careers and may need a further boost or a door opened to them again, perhaps after taking a few years out to have children. At this point, the option to spend a year attached to a theatre as an associate could prove invaluable in not just keeping them in the game, but acquiring the skills for their CV that would eventually put them in the running for an artistic-director post, should that be what they want. I know that associate roles already exist in theatres, but they are – not always but often – those that have the most opaque of recruitment processes of any staff roles in theatres. That's not to remove a theatre's freedom to appoint artists they particularly respect or want to work with to associate roles, but also to consider just how valuable these opportunities could be over time, in shifting the demographic of artistic directors we have in this country. If a critical mass of theatre companies – perhaps even as few as ten or twelve – started offering six- to twelve-month-long associate roles specifically targeted as directors returning to work after a period focusing on caring responsibilities that could, within five years, begin to create a tangible shift in terms of who our artistic directors are nationally.

There's also a huge opportunity to break down the traditional structure of having an artistic director and executive director coming up through set routes then working in tandem yet separately, responsible for their respective sides of an organisation. We could be far more fluid about what these roles are, seek out greater opportunities for crossover between them, and decide on the form that leadership should take on a case-by-case basis. Part of a board's responsibility when recruiting for executive-level roles should first be considering what are the many different models of leadership they could be open to, rather than jumping straight to advertising for someone who fits the mould of the person who's about to leave. Our theatre organisations are so broad and varied and it's odd therefore that so many of them share the same leadership model; surely there are as many different ways of structuring leadership as there are types of theatre companies? Breaking down the rigidity around the type of track record, career trajectory and profile we expect a person to have before becoming a credible artistic director is one of the things most likely to change the balance of the people who are getting those jobs.

These are just starting ideas. There are a multitude of others out there just waiting for us to conceive of them. Changing the make-up of our artistic directors won't be easy, nor will it necessarily be a quick win. But if we are looking for pressure points across the industry – places where, with a bit of effort, a far greater change can be initiated – then surely targeting our energies on broadening the range of people who get to set the tone of our artistic output is an obvious place to start. And if, in the process, we have cause to better examine, understand and build on the successes that theatre has already had in advancing women in administrative leadership, so much the better.

Young People

After founding Tonic it quickly became clear to me that many areas of theatre presented themselves as needing our attention. Choices would have to be made; we simply didn't have the capacity to do all the work that needed to be done. Knowing that it was necessary to make pragmatic decisions about the best places to start, I became intent on locating those particular areas where, with a bit of effort from Tonic, the greatest impact could be achieved. These I dubbed 'pressure points': places where the investment of Tonic's limited time and energy would return – progress-wise – the biggest possible return. It was like having a stone and knowing that if I threw it at one part of a pond there would only be the tiniest ripple, but if I went for somewhere else, and threw the same stone with the same level of force, the ripples would reach out far wider and would be felt much more broadly across the entire pond.

Given that none of us who want to engage in change-making work have unlimited resources, looking out for these pressure points can be a really good way of ensuring we're targeting our efforts in the most productive ways possible. In this section I'll spend a bit of time focusing on what, to me, is one of the clearest and most important pressure point we have: young people.

When it comes to achieving greater gender equality in theatre, it's difficult to overstate the importance of focusing our efforts around young people. Because if we change what they think today, that will change what our industry looks like and how it behaves tomorrow. The next generation of writers, directors, producers, performers, designers, administrators, technicians, educators (not forgetting audience members) are currently to be found in youth theatres, school drama classes, community-theatre groups, and further- and higher-education drama courses across the country. If we can change the way they, at a formative stage, perceive the role that women can play in drama and the theatre-making process, and if we can equally empower girls and boys to be part of all areas of theatre, we stand the best possible chance of changing how our industry will behave going forward. This is about leading change by targeting the grassroots so that, over time, change travels upwards and outwards through the system as these young people progress through it.

A striking mismatch

Even before setting up Tonic I'd been intrigued by how the situation could be improved for young women who are interested in theatre. My own background was in part working in theatre education, and I spent several years as a youth-theatre director. Consequently I had long been familiar with the scenario of turning up at the start of a new term to find a rehearsal room full of eager young people (at least 70 per cent of whom would generally be female), but despite scouring the shelves of bookshops and libraries I perpetually struggled to find scripts that responded to this high proportion of female participants. All too often the available options had just one or two good female roles, but nowhere near enough to give opportunities to all the girls who wanted to take part. I felt uncomfortable with the idea of asking girls to play men term after term simply because I couldn't find a script that was a better match for them. I knew that asking the boys to wear dresses, or play characters called 'Susan' or 'Mary' wouldn't be tolerated – unless done for high comedy – so didn't see why I should ask the inverse of the girls. Besides, I wanted to explore plays about female stories *as well as* plays about male stories with these young people. But I repeatedly found accessing the former far harder, despite how clear the enthusiasm was for theatre among the girls.

It was a situation that troubled me. By routinely staging plays with a noticeable lack of female characters (and, in particular, a lack of female characters driving the action on stage, rather than being on the periphery of it), sent dangerous messages to the young people taking part – both male and female – that women and their voices don't deserve a place on a public platform. Didn't it say that women's stories aren't worthy of an audience's attention? Being in a play as a young person can be a really big deal, a formative experience in some cases, and one that can create memories which endure for decades. So given that taking part in drama can play such an important part in a young person's life, I was concerned to think that for many of them – simply because they happened to be female – the message they might have received upon showing up was: people like you aren't very interesting.

100 Great Plays for Women

It took a few years for me to stop seeing this as a nuisance and start to see it as something that I, offering just one part of the jigsaw puzzle, could contribute to changing. The initial idea behind what eventually became my book *100 Great Plays for Women* was, at its genesis, a simple list of plays with predominantly or exclusively female casts which – so my thinking at the time went – I could research and then circulate among schools, youth theatres, and drama schools to help teachers, tutors and directors like me who repeatedly found themselves facing the problem of the imbalance between the number of girls who wanted to take part and the roles available to them. In the end the list never took shape – in that format at least; I was encouraged by industry colleagues, when I began having conversations with them about my idea, to see it as something that would benefit the professional theatre world too, and for that the permanence and weight of a book felt more likely to gain traction than a few sides of A4. When Nick Hern Books agreed to publish it, I realised that its reach could be far greater than anything I could achieve alone through a simple list.

Despite the change of format, the intention remained the same. The mission of *100 Great Plays for Women* was not only to *increase* the number of roles available to girls and women to play, but also to *widen* the variety of those roles. I tried, across the hundred plays I included in the book, to select a mix of style and genre, scale and subject matter, to provide a smorgasbord of roles for women to play, rather than just the familiar tropes of ingénue, dotty elderly aunt, chirpy prostitute, passive victim or buxom barmaid. It felt important that the people who encountered these plays – and especially the young people – got the chance to encounter women and their stories in the many different hues and varieties in which they exist in the real world, rather than through the oddly narrowing filters that drama has, historically, tended to apply to the female experience.

The specific needs of the youth-drama sector

100 Great Plays was a big success and has, the feedback I've received suggests, done what it was intended to. But, as far as young people went, I remained aware that the work for Tonic wasn't done there. Few of the plays in *100 Great Plays for Women* were written specifically with younger actors in mind. While many of the plays in the book can be performed by youth-drama groups, I know from experience that if you're working as a director with young people there can be certain things that you're looking out for in a play which those written for performance in a professional context don't always deliver. Often (although not always) you need large-cast plays, sometimes with as many as twenty or thirty roles – a type of play few theatres can commission today because they are so expensive to produce; you're seeking out material that is age appropriate; there can be requirements around the form and style of the piece (whether, for instance, the casting is flexible enough that it can concertina up and down as you either lose or gain young people over the course of a term); and for something that feels achievable to produce in the short or fragmented rehearsal time frames that many youth-drama groups work with (rehearsing a play one evening a week is a very different experience to four weeks full-time in a professional rehearsal room). I felt that there should be more plays written specifically for young actors to perform that placed the stories, voices and experiences of girls centre stage, and ticked these practical boxes for their teachers and directors too.

I'd already begun thinking about this before finishing *100 Great Plays for Women*. In fact, part of the way through writing the book Tonic was founded and, trying to pin down what the organisation should do and how, I held on to my theory of pressure points and decided that youth drama was a very good place to start. I was keen to get a clear picture of what the state of play was for girls taking part in drama, and so one of the first things Tonic did as a newly formed organisation was to conduct a nationwide research study on the experience of girls participating in youth drama, focusing on the quality and quantity of roles available to them. Over several months in 2012, and working in partnership with the National Youth Theatre of Great Britain, Company of Angels (now Boundless Theatre) and Zendeh, Tonic connected with people the length and breadth of the country who were involved in youth drama; we spoke to young people who were participating in youth drama (a big umbrella term we used to encompass membership of youth-theatre groups, participation in extra-curricular drama activities, such as lunchtime drama clubs and end-of-term school productions, attendance at part-time stage-school classes, membership of college and university drama societies, participation in community-drama projects such as summer schools); their teachers, drama tutors and youth-theatre practitioners; and – because we were interested in tracking the long-term impact of taking part in youth drama – adults who had done drama when they were younger (some of whom had gone on to work professionally in the performing arts, and some who had not). Through conducting focus groups, in-depth interviews and online surveys, we sought to build up a clear sense of what doing drama means to young people, what the possible benefits of it are and, specifically, whether these benefits were harder for girls to access and what the impact of this was.

Swimming in the shallow end

If this research sounds interesting to you I urge you to read the full report, *Swimming in the shallow end* (you can download it at www.tonictheatre-platform.co.uk/about/why), but I'll give an outline of some of the findings here. Although I'd been working in youth theatre for years, had directed and taught in drama schools, and – at the time – wasn't all that long out of a drama degree myself, the results were still fascinating. Certainly there were some things that weren't surprising and confirmed suspicions I had had. For instance, statistically, far more girls take part in youth drama than boys (75 per cent of just under three hundred teachers and youth-theatre practitioners surveyed nationally described their group as entirely or predominantly female, compared to 20 per cent that had roughly equal numbers of boys and girls and just 5 per cent that were entirely or predominantly male). Likewise, I hadn't been alone in struggling to find scripts that catered successfully to this volume of girls. Overwhelmingly, we heard, girls face a 'double whammy': not only are there far more of them in the first place competing for roles, but the number and quality of female roles are so reduced that what's left for the girls are pretty slim pickings. As one youth-theatre practitioner we surveyed, whose comment gave the report its title, said: 'Because fewer boys participate, their experience is often more positive. Couple that with the inherent sexism as regards the number of female roles and the portrayal of women in theatre generally, and the girls are definitely swimming in the shallow end.'

But beyond confirming that an imbalance does exist, there was also plenty that the research threw up that really gave me pause for thought and, if anything, strengthened my resolve that this was a subject Tonic had to work to improve. Much of this came from interviews and focus groups I conducted with young people, male and female. I was struck, for instance, by how many of the girls said that even when they had encountered female roles, how disappointing they had found them, considering them to be outdated stereotypes of femininity which they, as modern young women, struggled to connect with or feel excited about embodying on stage. I'd do an exercise in some focus groups where I'd ask the girls to write down three words they would use to describe themselves, followed by three words they'd use to describe the last character they played on stage. All too often the first set of words were along the lines of: 'bubbly', 'determined', 'focused', ambitious' and 'energetic'; and the second: 'drippy', 'silly', 'floaty', 'boring' and 'weak'. Of course, acting is all about pretending to be someone who isn't like you – that's the whole point of it. But if the people you're always asked to embody are repeatedly less than you – less dynamic, less intelligent, less interesting, less complicated – eventually that must begin to affect the experience you are having, and not in a positive way.

The girls spoke about their aspirations for the future, saying they didn't consider themselves secondary to men and that, as far as they were concerned, equality should be their right. But they were also painfully aware of the double standards imposed on women and girls across society in terms of physical appearance, behaviour and the extent to which they are encouraged to be vocal publicly. In terms of how this translated to their experiences doing drama, they frequently expressed the opinion that their physical appearance dictated and severely limited the nature of roles they would be considered for, in a way that wasn't the case for their male counterparts; they spoke about how never getting cast or only ever in small parts – not necessarily because they didn't consider themselves talented or hard-working but because they were one of a sea of girls turning up to audition – is soul-destroying, particularly as they watch boys who are less committed and not necessarily as capable repeatedly walk into proper roles. They observed that having too much to say – whether in rehearsals or in a devising process – could get a girl branded 'bossy' or 'big-headed', and so being quiet and keeping your ideas to yourself could be a better way of being accepted, on a social level, by the group.

While the boys spoke about their involvement in drama as being something that had increased their self-confidence – one describing his experience as having a 'snowball effect' on his confidence as he successfully moved on to more and more and bigger and bigger roles – the girls often said the opposite. Instead they spoke about a gradual erosion of confidence as, term after term or production after production, they either didn't get a part or were once again in the chorus or ensemble, despite how much effort they felt they had put into preparing for an audition, or how committed they had been to their drama group. While playing lead roles wasn't something the girls necessarily always wanted, they did say that playing a role that in some way impacts the action – and playing it well – is something that builds confidence. It demonstrates the trust your teacher or youth-theatre director places in you. It raises your status in the group and buys you the ability to have a greater say in the shape of the end product. It means you're getting the chance to try out how your voice sounds in a public context, but from within the safety of someone else's words. It delivers a sense of achievement if it goes well and can leave you thinking to yourself, 'I did it! Now what shall I tackle next?' For the girls, accessing these confidence-building benefits of youth drama seemed difficult, something I found interesting considering how frequently drama is described as a great tool for building young people's confidence (which undoubtedly it can be, but only if used well). As a side note: I frequently attend conferences and events on women in the performing arts and, in conversations attempting to explain the lack of women in senior roles, I hear the word 'confidence' (or at least women's lack of it) come up again and again as a key reason given to explain current imbalances. Given that the overwhelming majority of people who work in theatre will have taken part in drama when young, I wonder what patterns get put in to place around confidence there which, years on, may still be playing a role in terms of how we present and think about ourselves.

Finally, there was a conversation that happened in just about every focus group I ran with girls which has really stayed with me. The focus groups were always single sex, either all boys or all girls, but identical sets of questions were always asked of both groups. One question would involve me asking the young people to tell me about a time they hadn't got a role in a production they had wanted: how did it make them feel and what did they do about it? The boys, while noting this had rarely happened to them, said their feelings of annoyance and disappointment had led them to be proactive – they'd initiated conversations with teachers and youth-theatre directors to request an explanation or, recognising that as boys doing drama they were precious commodities, had simply moved to a different youth theatre so they could get a role there. This was a freedom it seemed the girls didn't have. Being, as one described, 'ten a penny' in youth drama, they expressed the same disappointment as the boys at the experience of not getting a part they wanted (or, as was more often the case with the girls, a part at all), except they had little option but to sit it out and hope the next production would be different.

At this point, the mood in the focus group inevitably became rather subdued as the girls articulated and then reflected on these frequent disappointments. However, almost without fail, at this point one girl would rally and, with what appeared to be an attempt to inject buoyancy back into the room would say something along the lines of: '*But* you've got to be grateful to be involved at all. Even if you have just one line, you've got to be grateful that you've even been given the chance to get up on that stage.' This would generally be met by much agreement from the rest of the girls and a general affirmation of how wonderful being in a play was and how lucky they were to even get close to such a thing. I found it touching how determined they were to remain positive in the face of what they recognised to be a glaring inequality, and yet it was concerning too. What was it about the 'show must go on' ethos of theatre that was teaching them at such a young age not only to accept the crumbs off the table, but to do so with a smile on their faces? It was such a markedly different response to that shown by the boys, and the acquiescence that the girls had seemingly learned at such a young age was troubling.

Platform

Tonic's response to our findings was to initiate a scheme called Platform. Through Platform, a partnership with Nick Hern Books, we commission and publish new plays that are written with young actors in mind, which have big casts and which, crucially, contain lots of brilliant female roles, not just one or two. In fact, stipulated in the writers' contracts is that the plays must have a majority or entirety of roles that are female or could be played by any gender, and that the scripts should place girls' voices, stories and experiences at the centre of the action. The first three scripts in the series were published in summer 2015, and to date the response has been exactly as I had hoped and anticipated: all three have been performed repeatedly by schools, youth theatres, universities, colleges and drama schools the length and breadth of the country, as well as in destinations as far-flung as Australia and the USA. In addition, copies of the scripts have been purchased by schools and youth-drama groups in Canada, Germany, New Zealand, Poland, Portugal and Turkey. Because we've targeted our efforts at publishing the scripts once we've commissioned them, rather than staging them ourselves, their reach has been far greater: yes, we could have teamed up with a youth theatre here in London to stage them, but how would that have reached the radar of young people in Aberdeen or Truro or Omagh?

The next two plays in the series are being written as I write this, and beyond those the plan is for Tonic to keep commissioning more plays year after year so that, over time, we are building up a new canon of outstanding writing for young actors, one that gives the girls plenty to get their teeth in to and plenty of options in terms of the kinds of roles they are getting to play. Of course, the aspiration is that the boys' roles will always be great too in the scripts, and I hope that young men performing in a Platform play will have just as enriching and engaging an experience as their female counterparts. But it is giving youth-drama groups the option of putting stories on stage that foreground the female experience, as well as stories that fore-ground the male experience, that feels so important. And it is vital that young men, as well as young women, get to see female characters leading narratives.

Beyond performing

I appreciate that I've focused almost exclusively here on young people encountering drama through performing, and that this isn't how all young people come to theatre. Some find their entry point through lighting it, stage-managing it, writing it, or various other ways. I'm aware too that, if you're reading this and you don't ever work with young people, you may be thinking, what's this got to do with me? But that, I think, comes back to the idea of messages and some of what was touched upon in the chapter on unconscious bias.

In that section, I spoke about how we all pick up on messages around us the whole time, and this feeds into how we feel about ourselves, as well as how we feel about others. The same stands to reason in theatre and the messages we give out. If, when encountering drama through the plays they study at school or watch at the theatre, the role of the female characters is more often than not peripheral, there is a message there for the young people about the legitimacy of women's voices and who the public is and isn't interested in listening to. Likewise, if a young woman routinely passes their local theatre and almost only ever sees male directors, writers or other creative-team members named on the posters outside, that sends a message about the range of roles that they – should they be interested in theatre – could do. You have to 'see it to be it' is a phrase that sums up this principle well – that becoming something, or taking on a certain role, is far easier if you have seen someone who's a bit like you doing it. So if, as a young woman, you've never see a woman conductor, that doesn't mean it's impossible for you to become one, it just means you are perhaps less likely to consider that it's something you could. If you're a young woman with a passion for acting but you never see women with your body type, or of your ethnicity, or with your accent, playing the kind of roles you would aspire to one day play, that may make it harder for you to visualise yourself achieving that dream. It perhaps means you won't even attempt to take yourself in that direction in the first place.

I believe that the reason for focusing on young people is even greater than the benefits of changing the theatre industry alone. Most young people who are involved in drama do so with no intention of ever working in the professional theatre, or even becoming regular audience members as adults. Regardless of this, institutions – both educational and arts-based – across the country put vast amounts of energy into providing young people with the opportunity to learn about and participate in the act of making theatre. This is done because, collectively, they recognise that experiencing drama has a value that extends far beyond those to our industry. Ask most drama teachers, youth-theatre directors and applied-arts practitioners why they do what they do, and relatively few will say it's about getting their young people into the industry (although having taught someone who eventually becomes a successful theatre professional might be a gratifying bonus). Most do it because they want to produce good citizens or to give their young people a great start in life.

They have recognised the values of drama in sending young people out into the world feeling emboldened, empowered and empathetic towards those around them. So it's a duty for all of us to ensure that every young person has a chance to access these benefits, regardless of their gender.

Self-awareness and Self-monitoring

In the early days of Tonic, as part of my efforts to work out how we could best serve the theatre industry, I decided to spend some time looking into earlier schemes and initiatives that had been targeted at increasing diversity in the arts. I wanted to learn from what had gone before. While it was incredibly heartening to learn about the successes, more often than not the change much of this work had achieved had been limited and short-lived. I wanted to know why that had been the case and what could be done better in future. What I learned could probably be the subject of another book entirely, but for now I'll focus on just one of the key reasons that presented itself. It has to do with the extent to which arts organisations are – or rather aren't – engaged in self-reflection and self-monitoring.

When looking at many earlier attempts at increasing represen-tation and diversity, I found that overwhelmingly they had focused on the underrepresented group themselves; what it was about those people that meant they weren't as engaged in the arts as others. So, for example, figures showing that a particular community was unlikely to visit a local art gallery might lead to an outreach programme, encouraging attendance from mem-bers of that community by inviting them to special taster sessions and family workshops. Or the disproportionately low number of musicians from certain demographics playing in orchestras might lead to the creation of networking and targeted training opportunities for young musicians. This work, seeking to reach out to and embolden underrepresented groups, was not without merit nor was it entirely unproductive. However, it represented only part of the equation. What these schemes almost never did was look at the institutions, gatekeepers or employers themselves. What was it about them – about how they worked, thought, communicated, derived their tastes, and assessed artistic quality – that was limiting diversity?

In fact, instances of institutions questioning themselves and their own practices appeared to be rare. What this meant was that the underpinning structures that created the conditions for the lack of diversity – what it was, for instance, about how an orchestra engaged with musicians that meant those outside one narrow group were routinely absent from their payroll – seldom got looked at, let alone questioned. It also created a false sense that it was somehow the underrepresented group who were to blame for their absence; that they were less committed, less talented or less interested, rather than recognising that it was the way things were organised that often represented the principle reasons curtailing participation. Going back to the analogy about a biscuit factory, it would be like me blaming a fig roll for not being a chocolate bourbon, rather than asking myself what it was about *my* production line and *my* approach to biscuit-making that led to such a homogenous output.

With this in mind, a key component of Tonic's work with organisations became about us encouraging them to think about themselves and how they work. Yes, to continue looking outwards, and to understanding what barriers may prevent members of a certain group from engaging in their work. But also to look inwards and to understand that this balance of looking both within their own walls, as well as outside of them, would yield the greatest results. This is something I would encourage any professional theatre company to do – whether it has a staff of two or two hundred – but I'd say it's just as valid an exercise for an amateur dramatic society, drama department, youth theatre, festival or any other theatre organisation to do. It's also something which, in their own way, individual theatre-makers can engage in.

Number-crunching

What does this look like in reality? Well, the first step, to take the example of a theatre doing this, is generally about encouraging them to gather detailed and concrete data on what they have been doing; actually getting them to count up how many men and how many women they have programmed the work of, or employed and in what capacities. Beyond undergoing the first step of a simple head-count, there are ever-deepening layers of complexity they can then examine to give themselves an increasingly detailed and revealing picture of what their situation is. So, rather than only measuring how near or far they are from a 50:50 workplace, they can monitor how they allocate their resources and attribute power within their organisation by assessing these things in combination with gender.

To give one example: a not-infrequent conversation I have with theatres is one in which they tell me how equal they have been recently in terms of the number of plays directed by men and women on their stages. And yes, if the data-gathering goes only as far as a tally of all female and all male directors that have worked for them in the last year then things can seem pretty equal. Encourage them to dig a bit deeper, though – to look at whether the plays directed by women are more likely to be in smaller studio spaces instead of the main house, have shorter rehearsal periods, fewer performances, smaller budgets attached to them, lower fees paid to the creative team, a smaller share of the marketing department's time allocated to them – and often a whole set of inequalities emerge which, in a simple head-count of male and female directors, had remained invisible.

Likewise, for all those organisations that describe themselves as 'very female' because so many of their permanent administrative staff are women, it can be extremely revealing to do some monitoring of what these women are being paid, how that pay compares to the hours they work each week (including the hours routinely worked above and beyond those in their contract), their length of time in post before receiving a pay rise or promotion, the size of budget they control and how many staff they supervise or line-manage – and then comparing that against the men in the organisation.

Number-crunching is an activity that can measure all sorts of things, not just employment or allocation of resources. A youth theatre may find it useful across the plays it is staging to track how many speaking roles there are for female characters – or in which female characters could be described as protagonists – compared to male characters, and then reflect on the extent to whether this matches the gender of its membership. Or a university drama department could examine how many texts by women are included in the reading lists it supplies its students, compared to those by men. Additionally, if looking at how many people of colour are included in its reading lists, how many of these are women?

It's often not until these numbers have been set down on the page that an organisation can begin to see where it genuinely is at, rather than where it *thinks* or *assumes* it is. When any environment has for a long time been homogenous, the arrival of a few people who are different to the prevailing group can seem so startling by comparison that a sort of optical illusion is created. It's easy to be tricked into thinking a sea change has taken place when, in fact, a look at the numbers will show us that, in percentage terms, the difference remains limited. Likewise, staging plays with one or two cracking female roles can give the sense that a cast is far more balanced than it actually is.

To show a little sympathy for all those already-stretched people out there whose shoulders this data-gathering is likely to fall on, I would concede that number-crunching in this way, especially when you're busy, can feel like a huge pain. It's time-consuming to set up a system for it, can open up thorny questions around the ethics of putting people in boxes, and is something that often feels antithetical to the freewheeling vibe I think many of us in the arts want our working environments to have. Breaking down the employment, opportunities and artistic output of human beings into numerical values can feel awkward, and there will be some steps in the process that are clunky and around which compromises must be made. It's an activity that will never be perfect. And yet, despite all this, and even with its faults, it's the bedrock of the self-reflection required in the theatre industry if we are to make progress towards gender equality. Without it, we won't have a sense of how much we've achieved, what there is left to do, or what are the priority areas for the targeting of our energies.

It goes without saying that it's only worth doing if done well. 'Oh yes, we monitor that for our funders' is something I hear a lot from organisations – and, yes, most of those in receipt of any kind of sizeable funding and especially public subsidy will be used to monitoring and reporting on diversity for their funders. However, ask them what they have noticed from their figures and there can be a blank; either no one has taken the time to check what the end figures are or mean, or the fields they have completed are so vague and broad that little useful information can be gleaned. Without exception, the instances

I have seen of organisations getting a lot from self-monitoring have been when they have designed their own criteria (while, of course, continuing to complete the monitoring information required by their funders). They will have thought long and hard about what information it would be useful for them to capture and what it is they're wanting to better understand about themselves and the people they work with.

Number-crunching is an activity it's all too easy to sleepwalk through; to mistake the act of collating the figures as the point of the exercise, rather than seeing it as a means to an end. It's the *analysis* of what those figures tell you that's the important bit. Given how time-consuming monitoring can be, and how revealing it can be when done well, simply going through the motions with it is a waste of time and resources. My hunch is always that, when people in the arts demonstrate a frustration with or lack of interest in data-gathering, it's because they've only ever seen it done badly: when it's been done as a way of ticking a box, rather than enabling genuine reflection on what they're doing.

Combining quantitative data with qualitative

Crunching numbers provides only part of the picture. In parallel with this work it is crucial to obtain the narratives behind these numbers which explain why they are what they are. What is needed therefore is a mixture of quantitative data (the numbers) and qualitative data (the narratives). If the terms 'quantitative' and 'qualitative' feel familiar to you, skip the next paragraph. If not, here's an example to explain them.

A council has recently taken a new approach towards encouraging local businesses to recycle and wants to conduct research into the effectiveness of this. To be most successful in understanding not only the *extent* to which their new approach has achieved change, but also *why* it was or wasn't successful, their research would need to obtain two kinds of data: quantitative and qualitative. The *quantitative* data is what would give them the numerical picture of how well they did, so, for instance, they may survey local businesses to find out the volume of material they recycled before and after the new measures came into place, and from that work out a percentage increase. The *qualitative* data would provide them with the story of why that percentage increase came about and would focus on hearing from people what – if anything – altered their behaviour. So this qualitative research may, for instance, take the form of interviews with a series of business owners, or focus groups with a range of their employees to find out why they either did or didn't start recycling. That's because, if the council discovers that the fact it started fining businesses for failing to recycle acted as a greater incentive than the posters it distributed extolling the environmental benefits, that would give it a very strong steer about how to achieve positive change in the future – and tell council members they should probably stop wasting money having posters printed. Had the council not obtained a combination of quantitative and qualitative data, it would have only had half the picture.

Knowing you've achieved change but not knowing why (all quantitative but no qualitative) isn't that helpful. Nor is hearing from people that things have changed, but not being able to measure to what extent (qualitative but no quantitative) – because without this knowledge you're unable to make an assessment about whether it's sensible for you to continue with your approach. You won't know whether the effort you're putting in is equivalent to the level of success you're getting out.

Similarly in theatre, understanding in a thorough, complex and, above all, useful way just what progress is or isn't being made in regards to gender equality relies heavily on not only conducting the quantitative research, but combining this with qualitative research. Counting how many people are taking part and how, even in quite a sophisticated way, won't give us the whole picture; it has to be understood in combination with the personal stories of the people those numbers represent.

Eliciting (and *listening* to) the stories of the people behind the numbers

As it stands, I would say this is something people involved in theatre are not very good at – surprisingly, given that our very trade is in speaking and listening! In fact, looking at theatre companies specifically, I'd say that one of the key reasons why many of the gender inequalities in our working processes persist isn't that most of us wouldn't want them to be eradicated, but just that we're not very good at really inviting and listening to feedback from people who have been affected by them. We all know to put out audience feedback forms and we write evaluation reports on the success of our work from the perspective of the outcomes. But how often do we stop to ask and to analyse not just the success of individual projects and pieces of work, but of *how* the work was made or the processes by which it was achieved? What is the impact of how we do what we do on the human beings who deliver it? And, given the precarious and fragile working lives of many people in theatre, how can we obtain this qualitative data in a way that is robust, sensitive, and yet unclouded by personal interest, fear or bias?

One of the biggest problems I've repeatedly observed in professional theatre is that we're largely split into two halves (although there are some people who fall outside of this) – freelancers and salaried staff – but that between these two groups there is often a lack of understanding and empathy. All too often, people on regular salaries simply don't understand the terrific pressure freelancers are under when working on a production: that they have an incredibly limited period of time to create a piece of work – generally from scratch, with a group of people who may not have met prior to the first day of rehearsals let alone worked together, in a building in which they may have previously barely set foot, and where the politics and culture are a mystery – and they must do this with such skill that people coming to see it will praise it to the extent that they will be offered the chance to repeat that process again, either there or somewhere else. This is because the success of that show, created as it is in highly imperfect conditions, is probably all that guarantees they will be in a position to pay their rent, or feed their kids, or still be in the game in a year's time.

Likewise, I don't think that freelancers always understand or appreciate the different yet equitable amounts of pressure that salaried staff generally work under: that the show currently in rehearsal is just one of countless pieces of work, projects and tasks taking up their attention, and that even if they wanted it to, it couldn't be the all-consuming, all-or-nothing sixteen-hours-a-day project it may be for the creative team. A theatre's staff can't necessarily make swift decisions or take abrupt changes of direction when the work calls for it, because they operate in a system much bigger and more complex, and requiring of more compromise, long-term strategy and plate-spinning than that of a rehearsal room. The interests or needs of the show may be at odds with the interests or needs of the organisation, and this is something they must navigate with care and diplomacy. Their loyalty to any one production must be matched by their loyalty to the wider organisation where, after all, they will remain once that group of visiting freelancers making the current show have packed up and left.

Overwhelmingly I would say the cause of this lack of under-standing and empathy is down to poor communication, which is interesting given that, on the whole, theatre people are particularly good communicators. There's generally a lack of feedback sought – theatres are too busy to seek it, freelancers too frightened or don't feel adequately empowered to give it – and what this means is that problems can persist. I'm not saying that every production should culminate in an *Apprentice*-style slanging match over who was responsible for the failure of the task. Rather that organisations – as the institutions that are often the gatekeepers of resources and opportunity – request open and honest feedback from the people they have bestowed these on.

Capturing the good news as well as the bad

Of course, data-gathering of this kind oughtn't be a purely negative activity. While I have been focusing on the failings that aren't always spotted, so too there are big successes going on in theatre the whole time that I think don't always necessarily get clocked, recorded or shared. This process of self-reflection should be about organisations monitoring what they have done well, not just what hasn't been a success. Knowing when staff, whether visiting or salaried, have been supported, enabled and empowered, or when artistic opportunities have been opened up to a wider group than was previously the case, is just as crucial as uncovering the bad stuff in order to understand how progress can be made. I've been talking about surveys and focus groups and feedback meetings, but that really is the most basic of approaches to this. There will be far more imaginative, exciting, and most likely fruitful methods by which we can extract information about what is currently going well and what could be done better. I also think this is something that could be a communal activity – so different organisations or perhaps even whole sections of the theatre ecology work together to capture and share information between themselves, and then support each other to reflect effectively on how they're doing. I don't think this is a pipe dream – the opportunity to work out how we are all going about doing this is there for the taking by some enterprising individuals.

Data-gathering for individuals

I want to finish off this section by noting that, while I've been talking up to this point about organisations, it's also something that's just as relevant for individuals (including freelancers), especially those that ever have responsibility for engaging others in work, offering contracts, or allocating opportunities to participants. To give one example: when I was working as a director I was very diligent about keeping lists of actors; both those I'd worked with and those I'd auditioned. I did this because it was something I was advised to do by someone when I was starting out – they told me how, particularly after several years in the job, it would be really useful to have an aide-memoire when casting. So I'd always diligently collated all the names of actors I'd auditioned or worked with into spreadsheets. One day I found myself noticing just how much longer the lists of male names were compared to the female ones. Although I hadn't initially compiled the lists with the intention of monitoring myself and my own casting decisions, seeing it laid out in front of me made me realise something that I subconsciously knew, but may not have clocked unless I had seen it written down like that: that despite my so-called feminist credentials and perception of myself as an equality-striving person, in reality when it came to whom I was personally responsible for giving work and artistic opportunities, the numbers didn't bear that out. And while I don't like to admit it, I'm sure that had I dug even deeper into those lists, to look not only at how many women I had effectively employed, but how many women above a certain age, how many women with a disability, how many women of colour, or how many women who hadn't come up through a conventional drama-school route, I would have found other similarly disappointing truths.

In this way, we all need to keep tabs on the choices we make – not only in regards to the other theatre-makers we work with, but perhaps also what work we consume, noticing if we haven't been to watch any plays by writers of certain backgrounds recently and then doing something to shift that balance. Constant self-monitoring can be hugely important in galvanising changes in our personal behaviour which, in time and cumulatively if enough of us are doing it, will affect the bigger picture. For me – and that moment looking at the list of actors' names played a part in this – Tonic began because I realised I had a level of complicity in a system I purported to dislike, and also a level of responsibility as someone who was privileged enough to have enjoyed the benevolence of the industry, to do something about it. I took it to an extreme and I'm not suggesting everyone now downs tools in whatever theatre job they're doing and sets up a gender-equality-focused organisation. What I am saying, however, is that each and every one of us who can, in some way or another, say we are part of theatre has, in our own way, a role to play in this.

This isn't something the industry needs to fix, because *we* are the industry. If things will shift it is down to us, *all* of us, to make that happen. We all need to reflect on how we work, how we think, and how we make choices. That's what will drive the greatest change.

3 About You

What tools can we use to create the change

About You

I began this book by clarifying that it isn't an instruction manual but a springboard for you to generate your own ideas for making change happen. Hopefully the previous section has given you plenty of food for thought about the many things, both big and small, that we as an industry could start doing to make things different – and the role that you, as an individual, could play in that. In this section we'll be looking at some strategies and some tools you can use to begin to turn your aspirations for change into tangible realities. As you start shaping your ideas, this final section of the book is intended to offer some thoughts on how you can target your thinking, how to be strategic, how to be sensible; essentially, how to give yourself the very best chance of being successful.

If we think for a moment about the process of putting on a show (in itself, an act of change: transforming words on a page into a three-dimensional live performance and doing so through enacting a series of discrete yet incremental practical steps), we can see that we give a great deal of thought to how we can provide ourselves with the best possible chance of achieving it successfully. For instance, we find a designated rehearsal space where the cast and director can work in a focused manner. We schedule all parts of the process, from the dates of the set-build to the timings of the tech, so that everyone knows when they need to have completed their part of the activity, and in what order. We work out how to communicate to the wider world, through press, marketing and social media, what it is we're doing so that the public knows to buy tickets and so we will have an audience. It's like putting a series of individual safeguards into place. Without any one of these safeguards being there, the show won't necessarily be a failure. But it does increase the chance of it being a bit of a hash.

The same goes for the work you're going to be doing now. The more things you can put in place that maximise your chances of being successful – the equivalent of providing a cast with a quiet rehearsal room rather than expecting them to work in the car park – the more likely you are to achieve the change you want. Nothing here is rocket science; these are all very common-sense things. But they're those that, having been involved in processes of change-making myself and watched others implement them, I'd most encourage anyone doing the same to consider.

What You Want versus How You Get It

First up, I'll draw your attention to understanding the difference between *what* and *how*.

I try as much as possible to meet with people who have got in touch with Tonic asking for a coffee and a chat, because there is a project or an enterprise relating to gender equality in theatre that they are trying to get off the ground. Often the reason they want to meet is that, having started, they've got in a bit of a tangle or recognise they have drifted off track. When I chat to them about their ideas in an effort to work out why this is, I often find there is a step to their thinking that has been missed out; they have jumped straight to the *how* without first working out the *what*.

What's the difference between *how* and *what*? The *what* is what you want to achieve. The *how* is how you're going to go about it. The common and easy error to make is to go straight to the how; to become seized with the idea for an activity of some kind – for instance, staging a festival of new short plays by women in a local theatre, or setting up an online network for female technicians – and, full of enthusiasm and excitement, to get cracking with making it happen. But if you haven't first articulated to yourself *what* you want to achieve, you can't be sure the *how* that you've landed on is the best possible approach. Making yourself slow down and be really clear on what you want to achieve is one of the best safeguards against you blowing all your resources on an activity which, although positive to do, ultimately won't create the change you want. It's also one of the best ways to ensure you're appraising the whole range of options open to you, rather than settling on the first that comes to mind.

To give an example: a drama lecturer on a course that routinely attracts high numbers of female students has an idea to set up a project in which each student selects a leading female theatre practitioner, researches them, and presents back to the rest of the group on their work and careers. This could be a really positive piece of work and a great way of raising the profile of successful women in theatre among a group of young people. But even so, it's a *how* not a *what*. If the lecturer were to take some time to question themselves on *what* they want to achieve (and ideally be able to state it simply and clearly in one sentence), they might say: 'What I want is for my female students to consider a wide range of careers in theatre for themselves, rather than just acting.'

At this point, having identified the *what*, the lecturer would be in a much stronger position to decide on the best approach as to *how* they might achieve this. The research project may still be high on the list because, by giving the students role models, it could encourage them to consider areas of the industry they had previously thought closed to women – or simply not known existed. But the lecturer may also find themselves considering other types of *how*s they could pursue. They may, for instance, recognise that alongside providing role models, giving their students opportunities to experience different aspects of the theatre-making process is crucial and so they could ensure that female students have the opportunity to, for instance, design the sound, or operate the lighting board, or compose the music for the next production. They may see, too, that breaking down barriers to the profession will be helpful in achieving *what* they aspire to, and so proactively seek out events where female theatre practitioners are talking about their work and encourage their students to attend. Or they might invite women from different areas of the industry to the college for career events or Skype interviews with their students.

Another example: I remember meeting an actress a while ago who wanted to take a one-woman show (which she would write and perform) to the Edinburgh Festival Fringe. Her acting career had been a long one, extending over several decades, and this would be her first foray into staging her own work. While the creative challenges of writing and performing her own material clearly appealed, the producing aspects of getting the show on in Edinburgh (not to mention the significant financial costs attached) daunted her. She appeared extremely anxious about them, seemed to be bracing herself for a significant financial loss, yet came across as having something of a kamikaze approach to taking a show to Edinburgh. She knew her show was likely to disappear without trace in such an oversaturated marketplace, understood the whole exercise would lose her several thousands of pounds and yet was terrier-like in her determination to do it regardless.

When I questioned her on what she wanted to achieve, she repeatedly said: 'To perform in a play I've written at the Edinburgh Festival Fringe.' But when we dug a bit deeper, it emerged that actually, that was a *how*, not a *what*. What, we worked out eventually, she wanted was: 'To have greater control over the artistic work I do.' Having hit the age bracket where the roles open to her felt like an ever-less-satisfying roll-call of aunts, elderly neighbours and grandmothers, she was craving creative experiences that were empowering and which put her as an older woman – and therefore the older women she would be portraying – at the centre of the action rather than on the edges. Once she had become clearer on *what* she wanted, the Edinburgh show revealed itself to be a *how*, and just one of a range of options available to her to achieve that. It also opened up useful questions around whether there were more effective ways of her pursuing her *what*, than throwing everything she had at one show on the Edinburgh Fringe. If she spun out her resources differently, for instance, by staging her work in a cheaper context she could perhaps do three or four shows in a row, thereby enabling her to achieve her desire for artistic control in a far fuller and more successful way.

Separating out the *how* from the *what* is one of the best ways anyone involved in change-making work can remain focused in their approach, and yet be open-minded towards the infinite possibilities that exist. It's a bit like the work that an actor does when using objectives or transitive verbs (actioning) to provide a framework for their performance. Knowing they're playing a speech with the intention of 'enlisting' or 'scaring' or 'praising' or 'reassuring' the other characters on stage, gives something concrete around which an actor can anchor their performance and yet still allows a huge amount of scope for them to play. By knowing *what* their character wants to achieve, they can go on stage every night and explore a different method *how* they can do this. The same is the case with creating change in any context – the possibilities are many and vast and, so long as you have a defined sense of what you want to achieve, you can have lots of fun playing with the many possibilities of how you will do it.

Focus On You

Whatever the change is that you want to achieve, the manner you go about it will be wholly dependent on you and what your unique skills, experience, personality and interests will bring to this. Whether the change you want to drive is big or small, you are the axle in the middle of the wheel.

It's useful, therefore, to spend some time considering the respects in which you are well-positioned, and less well-positioned, to contribute to making change. Everyone has different parts of the puzzle that they will be better or less well-equipped to take on, and it's sensible to be honest with yourself about what these are. What is it that you (and perhaps only you) could bring? Is there an aspect of this that no one else is covering and if so, could you be the person to do it? Is there good work happening somewhere that you'd be able to support? What, given your limitations, should you steer clear of?

An exercise you can use to help you think about this is to make three columns on a piece of paper, then at the top of the first write 'I have power over...', at the top of the second write 'I have influence over…', and at the top of the third write 'This is out of my hands…' Then, thinking about your current role or position, make a separate list for each. So, to use the example of a freelance casting director, they may write in their first column: 'I have power over which actors get auditioned by theatres'; in the second: 'I have influence over how a director thinks about a character' (a casting director can encourage a director to be open-minded about the sort of actor that might play a certain role – to consider, for instance, whether Mercutio could be played as a woman – but can't ultimately make casting choices on behalf of the director); and in the third column: 'What plays the theatres choose to programme is out of my hands.'

Straight away this gives the casting director a steer about where their energies could best be targeted and also where they would be less likely to yield results. If they've identified they have no say over what plays the theatres they work for produce on their stages, then spending time seeking out plays with big female casts probably isn't the most fruitful use of their time. But if they have power over something as important as which actors get through the door to an audition room, then this is a great place to start. They may, for instance, make a conscious decision to get to know the work of a range of actresses that between them represent a greater range of body types than are generally seen on stage. Then they can ensure that when they schedule a day of castings – and providing it doesn't directly contradict something in the script – the range of women coming to audition mirrors the breadth of women on an average street, rather than being representative of a certain narrow proportion of the population. Once the casting director has initiated actions in regards to those areas they have power over, they can move on to those they can influence; for instance, planting germs of ideas in directors' heads so they think beyond making the most conventional or traditional choices. Questioning, for instance, why Juliet should-n't be played by a size 18 actress, rather than, as is overwhelmingly the case, one who is a size 8. The casting director can't make this decision on the director's behalf, but may be able, by flagging it, to encourage them to see that casting a petite Juliet is a choice – albeit one often made on autopilot because it's what we're used to seeing – rather than a given.

Another tool that can be useful when considering the role you are best suited to play in driving for change is a SWOT analysis, a strategising tool that's commonplace in business, but I think works really well in this context too. SWOT is an acronym for Strengths, Weaknesses, Opportunities and Threats – and the exercise entails writing down what, when you think about yourself in the position you are in now, you would list under each of these criteria. Note that Strengths and Weaknesses are considered 'internal', i.e. they are about you: who you are, the qualities you have, and the things that you can control. For instance, a member of a theatre's technical team may list as a strength: 'I have a good rapport with my colleagues and am a team player'; and as a weakness: 'I don't always feel confident to speak up when I see behaviour I don't agree with.' Opportunities and Threats are 'external', i.e. they are things happening outside of you – and which you may not be able to control – but which impact you and affect your situation, either in a positive or negative way. So the technician may identify an opportunity as being: 'There's a new management team in place who are much more responsive to feedback from staff than their predecessors'; and a threat as: 'The way our shifts are scheduled means we rarely have time together as a department so don't discuss what isn't working well.' They would then, having written down everything they could think of in regards to their strengths, weaknesses, opportunities and threats, begin to notice where potential exists and where less so.

The activity of completing a SWOT analysis forces you to pay attention to yourself; it makes you consider what cards you have in your deck that could either help or hinder you. It's an activity that doesn't need to take you long – perhaps no more than fifteen minutes to complete from start to finish – and yet you often find that possibilities bubble up to the surface and pop into your conscious mind that hadn't previously occurred. After completing all four lists, the main activity is then to reflect back on what you've written. Take time to clock what you have on your side, what could be useful ammunition to you, and what the risks are that could undermine your success or which you may need to mitigate against.

Beyond thinking about your strengths, weaknesses, opportunities and threats, and what you do and don't have power and influence over, a final point that's worth noting here, and it may seem odd, is that sometimes things that are central to your identity or experience aren't those that give you the best platform on which to stage your fight. That's because if your detractors (and trust me, there will be detractors whenever change is in the air) can make the suggestion that your motives are questionable or that they are based on self-interest or are the product of sour grapes, they will. This is something that can seriously undermine your case, however well you put it together and make it. Sometimes, therefore, driving for change around an area that doesn't immediately affect you personally can be a good tactic for instigating shifts that will, over time, feed into something much broader.

To give an example: when my first book *100 Great Plays for Women* was published, I was invited to do lots of press interviews and to speak at various conferences and events about the book, and what the imbalance was in theatre that had prompted me to write it. Of course, I spoke about how damaging I considered it to be for men and women to be starved of access to stories about women (and the broadest range of women) on stage, but I also spoke a lot about actresses. I would flag that, as an industry, we train up and invest in generation after generation of actresses but then, overwhelmingly, fail to utilise them to anything like their capacity or give them the chance to return that investment to the industry as fully as they could. This is a subject which, were I myself an actress – unless I were a fantastically successful one – may not have carried as much weight coming from my mouth, even if the content of the argument had remained just as sound. As it was, as someone who has never acted professionally nor wanted to, I could speak up on behalf of my colleagues who do, and without anyone being able to make the 'There's plenty of work out there if you're good, if you're not getting work it's probably because you're not talented/not trying hard enough' argument in an effort to either dismiss or avoid engaging in the case I was making.

Considering how you can speak out on behalf of others is a very powerful thing to do when it comes to making change. If the male members of an amateur dramatic society are the ones who are most vocal about addressing the lack of roles for women in the range of plays the society has been staging, that's something that will – whether we like it or not – resonate more loudly than the identical argument being made solely by the women. That's because there is nothing, on a selfish level, that men gain from pursuing that agenda and so consequently it carries a great deal of weight. That's not to say this is about speaking for someone – or taking over, or preventing them from having a voice, and you must make sure that the manner in which you propose fighting someone else's corner is welcomed by them; rather, it is about you using what you have (which may be the fact you are *not* afflicted by a problem in the same way they are) and speaking or acting *in support of* others in order to contribute towards broader change.

In this way, thinking laterally or a step removed from your immediate sphere can often lead you to finding the most productive areas on which to target your energies. As an actress, for example, you may not feel capable of increasing the number of female roles that theatres programme (although I know plenty of actresses who do much-needed work lobbying on this front), but you might be brilliantly positioned to mentor young women coming up through the drama-school system or in youth theatres so that, by the time they enter the industry, they are robust and resilient. A female playwright may feel frustrated that work by women is not being produced to the same extent as work by men. But she may find that the most powerful way she can drive for change is not through speaking about this, but by using her influence to support, encourage and fight the corner of female directors proactively. Because, ultimately, if some of those directors she cheerleads for eventually move into artistic-director or associate-director posts, there is an increased chance that, in time, this will lead to shifts in the type of work being programmed by theatres.

Focus On Them

Sometimes the change you're seeking to initiate is purely in regards to yourself: to your own thought processes, actions and behaviour. But in other instances you will find you are seeking to encourage other people to change theirs. One of the best chances you can give yourself of being successful in this is by attempting to put yourself into their shoes. Try to imagine what, if you were them, would be your response to the change that is being proposed? What might make you feel negatively towards it and what might make you want to embrace it? What will it mean for you and what will you have to do on a practical, emotional and/or creative level to make it work? By considering why the people you will be targeting are currently doing what they are, and by empathising with what change will mean for them, you stand a far better chance of working out successful tactics for getting them to engage with your ideas.

You can't take it for granted that everyone will feel the way that you do about the change you are proposing. Nor that they regard the current inequalities you are seeking to redress in the manner that you do. Indeed, they may not even have noticed them or, if they have, not find them important enough to do anything about. This means that you need to be really clear in your communication on the subject. Don't assume that they have the same depth of understanding that you do; you may need to spell it out for them (alternatively, the sophistication of their understanding of the subject may far surpass your own!). You may need to keep a check on your emotions. Not everyone may share your rage at an imbalance you've identified, or the fizzing excitement you feel about a piece of change-making work you think should be conducted. Even things that may seem utterly common sense or morally indisputable to you may not to someone else. That doesn't necessarily make you right and them wrong; there will always be a multiplicity of takes on any one subject and a whole lot of grey areas in between. If someone doesn't share an identical worldview to yours, that doesn't mean you can't work together – with a spirit of compromise – and still make progress.

The more you can try to see things from other people's perspectives, the more likely you are to make an approach to them that is persuasive and compelling. So try to think: if you were them (and not you!) what might make you care about this? What might excite you about it? What might be your concerns and what would reassure you? Key to this is trying to identify what, for them, may be the benefits of engaging in this change-making work you are proposing. Are those benefits artistic (for instance, a wider range of work available to your audiences), commercial (I've spotted a way for you to make money), ethical (all the young people you teach should have access to opportunity, regardless of their gender), or social (this is about changing the way your audiences feel about the contribution women make to society) – or something else? In fact, are there mutual benefits you can identify so that, should you and they collaborate, there will be a win-win situation?

Respect other people's intelligence and creativity. And use it. This is what, as a director, I needed to do to ensure each production I worked on stood the best chance of being successful. However clear I may have been on the shape I wanted an actor's performances to take, I was never the one getting up there on stage doing it every night: they were. So my job as a director was to provoke, inspire, challenge and support them first and foremost to come up with the ideas for what *they* wanted to do on stage, and secondly to provide them with a practical framework over the course of rehearsals around which they could construct that performance. Occasionally, and if directly requested, I would give a really on-the-nose steer to an actor, but most the time I would try to avoid that, recognising the benefit instead of creating an environment in which they were invited to work out what to do because ultimately, they were the ones who – come opening night – would have to take ownership of their performance. If I had started telling the actors what the solutions were, rather than working collaboratively with them to discover these together and organically, at best I was going to have actors turning in disconnected and hollow performances: trying to please me, but not really understanding why they were doing the things they were. At worst I was going to have a cast walking out on me before we'd even finished rehearsals.

I think it's a similar principle when working with others to achieve change. *Telling* people what to do won't create change;

people have got to *want* to make things shift, and that is most likely to happen if they're excited about that challenge, are emotionally engaged in the subject, or are philosophically, artistically or intellectually intrigued by the possibilities. Value the skills and knowledge of the people around you, and remember: when trying to solve a problem of any kind, many brains on it are always better than one.

Be Strategic

Strategising can feel like a dirty word in the context of the arts, bringing with it associations of a Machiavellian, cold or corporate way of operating. But that's not the case. Having a strategy simply means being smart about how you approach the thing you want to achieve, and therefore giving yourself the best possible chance of being successful. To go back to the analogy of putting on a show, there is strategy in ensuring you don't wait until the first day of the run to start selling tickets. Or not working the actors into the ground before opening night so they're like zombies when you most need them to be fresh.

A big part of strategising is deciding how you are going to allocate your resources so that you are able to reach your goal rather than faltering en route. It's a bit like running a marathon having consumed the right amount of carbs before the race and then ensuring you sensibly spread out your water and glucose intake along the way; not having masses too much or far too little at any point. The resources you are likely to be allocating when attempting to drive for change may be your time, energy (both emotional and physical), money, and what you can get from your networks (if you are relying on people you know to do you favours, there are only so many times you can ask before that wears thin). Expending all your resources up front, or refusing to utilise any in an attempt to keep them all in reserve, may mean you either conk out before you've got to where you want to, or fail to get off the starting blocks. So you'll need to be balanced and measured in your approach. What, in the short, medium, and long term, can you realistically and appropriately dedicate to the change-making work you want to do? How will you be able to keep checking that you're on track with this? If the idea you have requires more of any resource than you currently possess, that doesn't mean you shouldn't pursue it, but you will need to build in additional steps to your plan, identifying where you will obtain them from.

Strategising is also about making decisions over what order you do things in. Do you, for instance, go straight for the jugular and attempt to reconstruct the way your department operates entirely? Or do you introduce small pieces of change gradually and incrementally, allowing people to get used to them before you go for the more seismic shifts? What's the first domino to fall, and is there one particular action that, if you enact it before others, will make leveraging further change much easier for you to do? If so, can you make this your priority? Is there a foundation you need to lay before cracking on with the actual change-making work? Perhaps a piece of research that demonstrates a need or illustrates what the benefits of change will be?

Identifying your 'low-hanging fruit' is an important part of this. These are people who you stand the best chance of enlisting to your cause because they're likely, for a whole range of reasons, to want to get on board with what you want. They're the equivalent of an apple that is well within your reach, growing on one of the lowest branches of a tree; you'd be a fool to ignore it (provided it's not mouldy and full of worms, of course), and instead put a load of effort into fetching a ladder so you can pick one from the very top. Identifying and winning over your low-hanging fruit is an important strategic first step. It means you've started, and can demonstrate that other people, not just you, are behind the idea of change happening. It may also be that they have connections with some of the apples further up the tree so that, in time, you can begin to bring them on board too.

Establish Guiding Principles (and Stick to Them)

As a director I always prepared really thoroughly. That's because I knew there would generally be a point in rehearsals when I'd become snow-blind; I'd be so immersed in the process and have so many different pressures on my time and attention that I'd lose sight of what I wanted the production to be. That's why preparing before starting rehearsals was so important. Just a note scribbled in a margin about what a scene or a moment should be delivering for the audience was often enough to get my overcrowded brain back on track.

A similar principle applies when doing change-making work. There will inevitably be times when you are so caught up or embedded in it (particularly if it is something you are personally invested in) that at a crucial moment your sense of clarity will desert you. At this point, having something to hand that brings you back on track can be vital in preventing you heading off down blind alleys.

I sometimes refer to this as establishing 'guiding principles'. In the early days of Tonic, if an opportunity came up for the organisation to be involved in a project, or to collaborate on a piece of work, my instinct would be to say 'yes' and throw myself into it.

But I soon learned that I needed to become far more selective about what I did and didn't choose for Tonic to do. There simply weren't the resources available for us to be doing everything that came our way, and if I didn't want to run myself into the ground, choices would have to be made. Establishing guiding principles was hugely useful in providing me with criteria against which I could make these – sometimes difficult – choices. They were:

- We never work alone, always in partnership with established organisations that have a wide reach.

- For the outlay of resources, the work we do has to have the broadest possible impact.

- The change our work is designed to do must be long-lasting, not temporary.

When any prospect came up I had to run it past the guiding principles, as if they were a checklist. If it ticked all of them, I could consider doing it. If it didn't tick every one, the decision was made: it wouldn't happen. At times this felt like a brutal process but, in hindsight, it was crucial for giving Tonic the clarity of intention it now has, and is possibly one of the main reasons we're still going (and growing) several years on. Without having cause to be targeted and selective I may have expired with exhaustion long ago.

Establishing guiding principles can be particularly valuable if there is a group of you working together to achieve change. Collaboration is great, and joining forces with friends or colleagues can be incredibly fruitful, but it's never without its challenges. Among any group there will always be differences of opinion, varying interests, and a range of perspectives on what the plan of action should be. This might mean that nothing gets done because no one can agree over where to start, or alternatively there is an initial burst of activity, but it's so diffuse and uncoordinated as everyone pursues their own individual ideas that little is achieved. Setting up guiding principles from the outset can be massively useful in reducing the risk of this. If anyone has an idea for a piece of work or an approach, the group runs it past the guiding principles. Only if it responds to all of them does it go through to the 'next stage' and get seriously considered.

A Change-Maker's Checklist

Nearly ready to crack on and create change? Here's a final checklist of things to focus on, to send you on your way.

Make it targeted

You can't solve everything; you don't have the time, energy or headspace (no one does). So decide what area(s), specifically, you are going to target, then set yourself a plan and a time frame for how you will work towards this goal. It might be something as simple as 'Each month read at least one play that I don't currently know by a woman written prior to 1950', or 'Proactively seek out six female lighting designers over the next twelve months, look at their portfolios, and meet them for a coffee.' If you achieve your initial goal, or find you can easily absorb it into your existing workload, great. Build on it and set yourself some more.

Make it measureable

If you can't track progress, how will you know whether you're achieving it? Find a way of taking a 'snapshot' of the situation you're aiming to change at the beginning of your work, and then continue to do so sporadically at predetermined periods after that, so you can compare and contrast. That may be about basic number-crunching, but there are other kinds of 'snapshot' and ways of monitoring progress too. You could, for instance, ask people how they feel about something and measure whether their opinions change over time, or observe behaviour and monitor whether it shifts and, if so, how?

Find your networks

You're not going to be able to do this alone. Whether you're trying to change the culture in your workplace, lobbying your local theatre to broaden its artistic programme, or have your eye set on creating an industry-wide revolution, you will need collaborators, supporters and enablers. Enlisting other people to join you in the change you're trying to make will be crucial, so work out who are the people you most need on your side, and be able to articulate to them what you want to achieve, why, and how they can be a part of it.

Do something you enjoy

If you're someone who gets a buzz from compiling spreadsheets: great, do it. If you find spreadsheets among the most boring things on earth, they're probably not what you should target your energies on. Remember that creating change can be a protracted and difficult process. If you pick a change-making activity you're not going to enjoy or that doesn't fire you up, you're far less likely to stick at it.

Know when to admit defeat (and change tack)

There is no shame in admitting that the approach you've decided to pursue isn't working. If you've been bashing your head against a brick wall for some time and getting absolutely nowhere, you're only going to give yourself a headache. So stop, regroup, and work out a new direction to head in. The main thing is not to let yourself get disheartened; you won't be starting from scratch when you embark on Plan B, because there will inevitably be learning and experience that you will be taking with you from your time working towards Plan A.

Look beyond theatre for inspiration

One of the theatre industry's biggest weaknesses is its occasional ability to be inward-looking and insular. This means we're not always open to innovative ideas, better ways of thinking, or approaches that could help us make the industry what we want it to be. Theatre is not the only industry that has ever had an issue with gender inequalities or that has wanted to create change. There's a whole world out there and parts of it are doing significantly better than we are. It doesn't take more than doing an internet search for 'gender-equality initiatives' to find boundless examples and inspiration. Let's take advantage of this great work that has gone before by learning from it.

Finally...

I've been working on this book on and off over the course of about two years. Even over that relatively short period of time, the situation for women in theatre has changed, and continues to change fast. There have been landmark productions and award-winning shows with women at the helm; there have been battles over how many plays by women are on the GCSE and A-level syllabuses; new female directors coming in to post (and, in some instances, departing too); an ever-louder public discourse about the need to put stories about women on our stages. The level of progress has been mind-boggling, widely positive and full of promise. Yet there remains so much more for all of us to do.

Tonic is a strange organisation, because our ultimate goal is our own obsolescence. My – possibly romantic – hope is that one day we'll no longer be needed, because the change we're pushing for in theatre will have been achieved. That's a long, long way in the distance – and we won't be the first, nor almost certainly the last, to try to get there. But if you were to ask me what total success looks like for Tonic, I would have to say: that it is no longer necessary for us to exist.

Likewise this book will, I hope, become less and less useful as the change it desires us to make becomes more and more established across all corners of our industry. Wouldn't it be wonderful if, in time, there were no more surprises for readers coming to these pages, no more actions that hadn't already been achieved, no more work to be done? Idealistic? Possibly. But as Rufus Norris says in his foreword to this book, theatre should be a brilliant example of diversity. So I say let's keep dreaming, and trying, and pushing, and innovating, and fighting until we are. Whether or not you believe theatre can change the world, working together to ensure environments exist that are open, inclusive, embracing of all, and function as beacons of equality and diversity cannot be anything other than a good thing to do.

So please get out there and make your mark on this big, puzzling, complex, intriguing and endlessly fascinating challenge that is redressing gender inequalities in theatre. If you find yourself wavering, or temporarily lose your way, take yourself back to the list you made during Part 1 when you answered the question: *Why is gender equality in theatre important to me?* Because, as I said then, *we* are the industry. If change is to happen it is down to each and every one of us to get stuck in and to revel in the challenge of making it happen.

So let's do it.

Get Involved

Have your own experiences to share?

Starting out on an amazing project?

Looking to connect with others
working for change?

We want to hear from you!

Continue the conversation
by following **@allchangebook**
on Twitter

And share your updates using
#allchangeplease

Acknowledgements

Thank you to:

Matt Applewhite, Tamara von Werthern, Jon Barton and everyone at Nick Hern Books. For commissioning this book and for being such brilliant ongoing partners to Tonic.

Arts Council England. Without support from Grants for the Arts, writing this book would simply not have been able to happen.

'Team Tonic' for making everything we are achieving possible: the endlessly wise Vicky Long, the endlessly patient Steph Weller and the endlessly supportive Board of Trustees: Craig Bennett, Moira Buffini, Eleanor Lang, Sita McIntosh, Sabina Mohideen, Mee-Ling Skeffington, Kirsty Starkey and Anna Vaughan.

Everyone in the New Work Department at the National Theatre Studio where Tonic was formerly Affiliate Company and where much of this book was written.

Rufus Norris for agreeing to write the foreword, even though he's one of the busiest people I know.

ACKNOWLEDGEMENTS

Friends and colleagues who went above and beyond in terms of listening to me complain about writing this book and helping me develop my thinking on it. In particular, Gilli Bush-Bailey, Charlotte Melia, Sabina Mohideen (who gets thanked twice!) and James Pearson.

Finally, and above all, to Edward. For everything.

TONIC

Tonic Theatre was created in 2011 to support the theatre industry to achieve greater gender equality in its work and workforces. Today, Tonic partners with leading theatre companies around the UK on a range of projects, schemes, events and creative works. While Tonic was created to achieve change in the UK theatre industry, it soon became apparent to us – and others – that the unique approach we had developed could be of use beyond theatre alone. Today we work across many areas of the arts and the wider creative industries.

Tonic's approach involves getting to grips with the principles that lie beneath how our industry functions – our working methods, decision-making processes, and organisational structures – and identifying how, in their current form, these can create barriers. Once we have done that, we devise practical yet imaginative alternative approaches and work with our partners to trial and deliver them. Essentially, our goal is to equip our colleagues in UK theatre with the tools they need to ensure a greater level of female talent is able to rise to the top.

Current and recent partners include: Almeida, Chichester Festival Theatre, English Touring Theatre, Headlong, National Theatre, Northern Ballet, New Wolsey Theatre, Northern Stage,

Royal Opera House, Royal Shakespeare Company, Sadler's Wells, Sheffield Theatres, Tricycle, UK Theatre, West Yorkshire Playhouse, Young Vic.

www.tonictheatre.co.uk